I Just Want to Be Happy

Healing Your Way to Happiness

Helen Murray

FIRST EDITION
ISBN: 9781772770513

PUBLISHED BY:
10-10-10 PUBLISHING
MARKHAM, ON
CANADA

Contents

This book is dedicated to my family with all my love
My husband Ken Batte
My children – Joni, Jami, Joe and Jerica Batte
My parents John and Amelia Murray
Jean and Ken Batte
My siblings and their spouses;
Debbie and Ron Simmons, Dianne and Brad Schieck,
Nancy and Gary Gibson, Alphonse and Crystal Murray
My nieces and nephews;
Tiffany, Vicki, Jesse, Kevin, Scott, Tamara, Shelby, Shawnee,
Sierra, Riley

Kevin Murray

And to friends
Karyn and Ron Hutchison
John and Cindy Redburn
Stu and Myrna Hutchison
Natalie Carere

For all of these people have been impacted in a way that changed
their lives drastically from the loss of a young person; some a child, a
sibling, a nephew, a cousin, or a friend.   The people named on this
page are all incredibly special people and have survived more
sadness and heartbreak than any person should have to endure. My
wish is for you to move past sorrow to living a life of joy. I have
included my favourite hymn as a tribute to you.
With love, Helen

Make me a channel of your peace,
Where there is hatred, let me bring Your love,
Where there is injury, Your pardon Lord,
And where there's doubt, true faith in You

Make me a channel of your peace,
Where there's despair in life let me bring hope,
Where there is darkness - only light,
And where there's sadness, ever joy

Oh Master, grant that I may never seek,
So much to be consoled as to console,
To be understood, as to understand,
To be loved, as to love with all my soul

Make me a channel of your peace,
It is in pardoning that we are pardoned,
In giving to all men that we receive,
And in dying that we're born to eternal life

Oh Master, grant that I may never seek,
So much to be consoled as to console,
To be understood, as to understand,
To be loved, as to love with all my soul

Make me a channel of your peace,
Where there is hatred, let me bring Your love,
Where there is injury, Your pardon Lord,
And where there's doubt, true faith in You

In loving memory of

David John Murray
Wade Evan Simmons
Laura Murray
Bodyne Hutchison
Tanner Redburn
Steven Hutchison
Alina Carere
Blake Fischer

Acknowledgements

This book has been a project of love and learning. I would like to thank my husband for all of his support; financially and emotionally. He provided me the freedom to do what I needed to do without asking questions, and for that I am grateful. This was not an easy project for me to complete, and there were many days that I spent the entire day writing and ignoring everything else, and he never complained. I would also like to thank my children, for it is them that have taught me so much about life. Their ability to be open and honest people who are able to share their thoughts so freely has encouraged me in many ways, especially while writing this book. The admiration I have for them is unwavering; they are some of the best people I have ever had the privilege to know. They are wise beyond their years, and more emotionally evolved than I could ever hope to be. Their pursuit of happiness and of a better life inspires me daily.

I would like to thank my parents for everything they have done for me; they have supported me and my family in so many ways over the years. They have, above all else, shown me the meaning of love. They have sacrificed tremendously over the years to provide for their family, and it wasn't always easy but they always managed. They have been my source of strength while raising my own children. My siblings have also been a great source of inspiration to me throughout life and while writing my book as well. It is my sincere wish that they can read this book, and understand this is my account of the moments in my life, and I am not assuming that they would have the same accounts of those moments in their lives, for we are each very different people. I hope they can enjoy my book and find something within the pages to help them release some of their own pain.

I would also like to thank all of the incredible women I had the honour to work with in my previous positions. The opportunity to get to know you and to learn from you was amazing, and I wish you all the very best in life. I know that you will succeed in life as people and as professionals, but remember to take time to take care of you! Each of you has taught me something about human nature, about dealing with people, and about myself.

I have a special thank you for my previous boss, Bruce Stokes, as without his influence in my life, I would not be where I am today. I am grateful to have had the opportunity to work with and learn from you. Your belief that I could grow and expand my business acumen has encouraged me to become more and do more than I previously thought possible. You also taught me that I am worthy of financial freedom, and that trading hours for dollars is not the way I want to live.

To Gregory Downey, my everlasting gratitude, as you helped me see the person I could be, and should have always been. You showed me how to let go, how to forgive, and how to cry. I wish you the best and know without a doubt that you will achieve your own greatness! To Raymond Aaron for helping me get my book done, and for his support during the process and for showing me that it is okay to want more from life and how to get it, thank you! I thank Joe Vitale, Tony Robins, Jack Canfield, Bob Proctor, Sonia Ricotti and the late Wayne Dyer for their work in the field of self-development as they have all improved my life in ways I could never have imagined. Their knowledge and commitment has allowed me to learn so much, and to continue my own personal growth, and I am eternally grateful to be able to learn from such inspirational people.

My deepest thanks and gratitude is to you who have loved and lost. My heart is with you and I sincerely hope that my book will help you in some meaningful way. Live, Love and Be Happy!

Canada's #1 Empowerment Authority
Helen Murray

Foreword

Helen Murray has tasted sorrow throughout her life several times, with her first heartbreak on the day of her 5th birthday, when her brother was hit by a car while riding his bicycle. She is no stranger to loss, as you will see in this book. *I Just Want to Be Happy* is the story of her life, and how grief and trauma changed her, and how she transformed back to living a life of emotional freedom. This is her life story from her perspective, and it has been written out of her deep desire to help you heal. Helen is a Certified Life Coach specializing in helping you overcome trauma through loss. It is her sincere hope that by reading her story you can now move from sorrow to joy while still remembering, honoring and loving your loved ones.

Helen's story is completely her own, but her experiences are relatable and her emotions will resonate with you, having suffered loss but lived on. The narrative has familiar elements of family stories all wrapped up in an intense love. Her story will connect with you, if you have lost a loved one, either family or friend, or have watched your parents, siblings, or children grieve a personal loss. She writes her story from the viewpoint of a child, a sister, a spouse and a mother, as she has experienced loss in all of these life stages.

Her story is an honest account of how loss and grief has impacted her life, and how it can impact your life in ways you may never recognize within yourself. She deeply examines how a person changes over time, and how grief can affect every facet of your deep subconscious level. She has exposed her own pain and suffering in an attempt to heal herself, and at the same time to reveal to you how grief can manifest itself and eventually take over your life, keeping you from living a life of peace and joy. Helen has said that her real purpose for this book and for her own transformation is to be able to give the gift of joy to you so that you can choose to examine your life and make changes to your own life choices. She believes that you can only change if you are shown other options. Her own family has been grief- and fear-driven for so long that it is passed on generationally, and it is her mission to show future generations that life should not be based from a place of fear, but rather a place of love and gratitude.

This book is an honest reflection of Helen's life, and a must read for you having suffered a deep loss that caused trauma and pain that has changed the trajectory of your life or someone you love.

Raymond Aaron
New York Times Bestselling Author

Introduction

I was born May 22, 1967. I was the fifth child in our family; I have 3 older sisters, an older brother and a younger brother. My parents were married young; my father was 20 and my mother only seventeen years old. After their marriage they moved west, where they lived from 1958 to 1962. Everything they owned was on a trailer they pulled west themselves. They arrived at their destination late at night, and parked the truck and trailer in a shed overnight. Sadly there was a fire in the shed that held their belongings while they awaited their house, and they lost almost everything, including most of their wedding gifts. Dad was already working on his uncle's ranch, the largest privately owned ranch in Alberta. They lived in a small shack, and it was here that they had their first two children, Debbie born in 1959 and David born in 1961. My mother was quite homesick, so finally she convinced my father to return to Ontario in 1962, while expecting their third child.

Dad came from a family of eleven children. My mother's family was much smaller; she had two sisters and they were raised in the Ripley area. However, her father died when she was 12, and her mother remarried in 1958. She now had a step-sister, and 3 step-brothers. My parents bought a farm in Holyrood, Ontario, which is where my dad's family was from. We lived in Holyrood for about five years until the farm well went dry. In an effort to save the animals and the farm, they hooked into another well across the road to be able to supply water to the animals. This ended up being the undoing of the farm as the water in the neighbouring well was bad, and it killed the animals. I was about six months old at this time, and became quite ill. It was discovered through my illness that the well water was contaminated with salmonella. Fortunately, I survived, but the animals were not that lucky. The loss of the animals crippled my parents financially and they ended up losing the farm. We moved to Palmerston in April, 1970, where we stayed only for a short time. In March of 1972 we moved again, this time to Drayton, a small village of about 700 people, where we stayed for about 7 years. This is where my memories really begin; I don't have many memories previous to this time in my life.

My parents have always been extremely hard-working people. My dad always worked long hours and did very laborious work. He often worked out full-time, ran his own farm and hired out his services to other farmers for crop season. He was out of the house before we were out of bed in the morning, and returned home long after we were in bed at night. He was always home for supper at 7:00 p.m. without fail though, as family time was important to both him and Mom. My mom was also a worker; she worked full time, raised six kids, kept the house, and previous to moving to Drayton also helped in the barn. Mom commuted to work before commuting was even a thing. She drove an hour each way to work and back, on top of her eight hour day, kids, house and farm work.

My mom had six kids before she turned thirty. In those days there was no maternity leave or pay. In fact, prior to 1971, the law prohibited employers from hiring women in the six weeks after they gave birth. Women therefore had six weeks at home with their baby, but it was without pay. Most working women had to return to work after the six weeks as they could not continue without their wages. Mom's commute was part of the reason we ended up moving to Drayton; it was a much shorter commute for her. Mom worked at Midwestern Regional Centre, a large facility for the mentally disabled. Dad also found better work in Drayton than he had in Palmerston; he was a hired hand for a large farm and earned $500.00 per month plus a house. The house was a wonderful old yellow brick farmhouse with a veranda on the main level and a balcony on the upper level. It was a large farm with lots of trees, fields, and luscious grass. We had lots of room for our ponies, horses, calves, dogs, cats etc. When you are raised on a farm, animals are a big part of your life, but I feel it was even more so for my family.

My oldest brother, David, was diagnosed with rheumatoid arthritis at age seven. He was unable to walk, and the doctors told my parents that he might never be able to walk again. Sadly, there was not a lot that could be done for him; he was able to have baby aspirin to help alleviate the pain, and that was all the treatment that was available for him. He spent a number of weeks in the hospital at age 7, and then again several more weeks when he was about 10 years old. David had an old Shetland pony named Molly, and a new pony named May. Horses were a huge part of both Dad's and David's lives. Dad had given May to David, as Molly was getting quite old. When David returned home from the hospital, he refused to give up. Even though he was unable to walk, he crawled to the barn every day on his stomach, just so he could get to his ponies. He somehow managed to get himself up onto his pony and they would go riding for hours on end, all over the countryside. He was a stubborn one but I think this determination is what kept him going. His determination and strength was incredible and there is no doubt in my mind that his own strength is what cured his rheumatoid arthritis. David was quiet; just one of those endearing types that people are drawn to, but he had a quiet determination about him as well. He did walk again and actually went into remission by the time we moved to Drayton, and was finally living a normal life.

Family was extremely important to both of my parents. Even though they worked long, hard hours, they somehow made time for us too. We were certainly expected to pitch in and help both in the house and in the barn, and we all had daily chores and responsibilities. My parents were strict, and there were many rules, but they also believed in playing and having fun together as a family. We often danced to the radio in the living room after supper and dishes were done. My dad was a fabulous storyteller and would act out stories in a very animated way rather than reading them from a book. He was especially good at Peter Pan. We much preferred his versions to the actual book version when mom would read to us. Life was good in those days. Everyone worked hard, played hard and laughed often!

Chapter 1

The Tragic Moment

May 22, 1972 was a beautiful, sunny, warm spring day, and the day of my fifth birthday. It was shaping up to be a perfect day. My mom had arranged a birthday party for me as we had recently moved to the area and I would be starting Kindergarten that fall. She thought it would be good to have a party so I could meet some of the other kids before I started school. The house was busy and happy that morning as mom was baking a cake and getting the house ready for the party. All hands were on deck preparing for my special day. My dad was working and my baby brother was only ten months old, so they were both excused from the work.

My guests arrived early in the afternoon, some just dropping kids off, others staying to chat for a bit. We spent our time outside playing leap frog, catch, tag, and hopscotch; all popular activities for kids back in 1972. My older siblings were organizing the games, keeping things moving, and watching us play. We lived on a farm so there was lots of room and lush green grass. It was your typical five year old birthday party and things were going nicely. Everyone was getting along and we were all getting to know each other.

At some point my mother was in the house getting things ready and realized she was out of pablum for the baby. She called my oldest sister and brother into the house and gave them instructions to go into town to the grocery store and purchase a box of baby cereal. We lived quite close to town and it was nothing out of the ordinary for the kids to walk to town and do small errands. For some reason my brother said he would go alone and that there was no need for my sister to go with him. Again, this did not seem to be strange at the moment, and since we had a house full of guests my mother agreed, so my brother headed off to town on his bike. It was a short trip and he would be back quickly. My mother continued on with what she was doing inside, and the party continued on outside.

There was lots of laughing and giggling, and the laughter and enjoyment of the day could be heard throughout the yard and into the house. It's been so many years now that those memories have faded. To be honest, I don't really even remember who was at the party, or really many particulars about the day, but I can remember all of the feelings of that day very clearly. It was a happy day, one of the last that I can truly recall being filled with fun, laughter and joy.

Suddenly, from out of nowhere there was a terrible sound. It was so loud and so close that we all immediately stopped whatever we were doing to look and see where the noise had come from. People came running from everywhere, my mother from inside the house, and kids from every corner of the yard. People were screaming, yelling, crying…there was so much noise and confusion! Down the laneway and across the road there had been a terrible accident.

I am very unclear on the exact events and how exactly things played out for the remainder of that day. I know my father appeared from out of nowhere, I know that someone came to our house to call all of my friends' parents and arrange for them all to be picked up and taken home. There was an ambulance, my parents left, and there was such an overwhelming feeling of fear and panic. Everything happened so fast! I don't recall who stayed with me and my siblings, if we went somewhere, or what happened at all really, after the initial shock.

My brother had been hit by a car. He was almost home with the baby's food. When we heard the crash and looked out to the road we knew it was my brother. There were no bike helmets in those days, so he was totally unprotected. He had been hit by a car, and it looked as bad as it sounded. We could see his bike, so we knew for sure it was David. Also, in those days no one had CPR training so there was no help for him until the ambulance arrived. Finally, the ambulance showed up and David was taken to the hospital, but it was too late. He passed away in the ambulance before they even reached the hospital. I think my mom rode in the ambulance with him, and my dad drove behind, but even that is fuzzy. Drayton was a very small village with no hospital so he was taken to Palmerston, the closest town with a hospital.

From here I really have no idea about time reality. I don't know how long my parents were gone, I don't know where we went or who stayed with us, and even as I write these words, I cannot put time into perspective. I know that at some point my parents returned home, my grandmother showed up at our house, and our house seemed to flood with people. I remember my Aunt Nancy coming to our house as well, but mostly all I know is that there were many faces drifting in and out of focus. I remember hearing conversations about a funeral, and plans being made. But even the events leading up to that are all very distant to my mind and I can't seem to grasp hold of the days and weeks that followed my brother's death. Thinking back seems as fuzzy and distant as those days felt to me then, 43 years ago. I do have one vivid memory, and that was of me and my sister Nancy at the funeral home. She and David had always been very close, kind of kindred spirits in a way. Nancy was a bit of a tomboy, and really the closest thing David had to a brother for many years. Nancy and I were standing in front of his coffin, and Nancy was about to reach out to touch his hand. She had never been to a funeral before and therefore had no idea how a dead person feels. I remember grabbing her hand and holding it, and trying to explain to her that David was going to feel very cold and hard. I remember thinking that I couldn't let her touch him without her knowing this first because I knew it would shock her and be too much for her that day. Thankfully, I had been to a funeral at age three. My mom took me to her grandmother's funeral, but not my siblings. My dad was against her taking any of us but in the end agreed that I could go with her since I was so young I would not likely understand what it was all about. Naturally though, a three year old is inquisitive, and while my mother, who was holding me, stood in front of the coffin, I reached out and touched her grandmother's hand. This is how I came to know how someone feels after they have passed away. To this day, I am eternally grateful that I had that experience as a three year old so that I was able to save my sister from feeling that shock ripple through her entire body as she touched our brother for the last time.

It's funny really; I had always seen my big brother as a "big" person. He was always so strong, smart and capable from my perspective. He always knew what to do, he was always there to help me, play with me, and he was always so kind and gentle to me. In all of the memories I do have of David, I never remember him being angry or upset with me. Certainly now I see this was strange as most siblings tend to fight with each other at least some of the time. He was such a huge part of my life, and now he is gone...forever!

May 22, 1972, was indeed the day my life changed. At five years old I knew that I would be a different person somehow, and that things would never quite be the same again. That was a tough time for all of us. My dad continued to work long hours, seemingly even more than before. My mom was very different; she was tired and slept most of the time. She didn't go back to work; I don't think she was able to leave us. The house was very quiet. There was no laughter inside our walls.

Of course, we all got up each day, ate our breakfast, completed our chores, and did the things that needed to be done, but that was about as much as any of us could do. My sisters still had to go to school, we continued to live, to work, to exist, but more than that was too much. My mom must have taken care of my little brother and me, but mostly I just remember the silence. Mom would lie on the couch and I would be her nurse. I would put cool cloths on her forehead and eyes for her while she slept. I sat by her, checking on her, and talking to her occasionally, but mostly she slept and I sat by her side. Things had to be very quiet as she needed her rest because her head ached so badly. Dad would come home each day for lunch and supper, and he would check on us and make sure we were all doing okay.

Time got back to normal. We got up at regular time, we ate at breakfast time, Dad was home at lunch time, the kids came home at normal time after school, barn chores and homework were done, Dad was home for supper time at 7:00, and bedtime depended on how old you were, but no one needed to be told to go to bed; everyone seemed to be tired. Bedtime would come but sleep would not, even though I was so tired. For a long time (I don't really know how long it went on) I would get back out of bed and slip quietly back downstairs. Sometimes Mom would read short bible stories to me while I sat on Dad's knee, and I loved the peace that it somehow brought me. My dad was always sitting in his big green chair, and I would climb up on his knee and finally cry myself to sleep. I always woke up the next morning in my own bed; each night after I fell asleep he would carry me back upstairs and tuck me into bed. This came to be one of my favourite parts of my day, and my favourite chair. These moments are the moments I cherish, the calm strength I needed to face the next day; the quiet time I was able to spend with my mom and dad, in solitude, and in safety. My dad's strength was incredible to me at that age. How he hurt so deeply himself, but always had the ability to take away my pain when I needed it the most. Sleep did not come easy, but it happened much better cuddled up on his knee with his arms wrapped around me in his big green chair.

> *"You'll feel guilty that you are still breathing.*
> *But you can't stop.*
> *You'll feel guilty for wanting to laugh again.*
> *And it will be awful the first time you do.*
> *You'll feel guilty for just about everything at first.*
> *And someday, at some point,*
> *You'll start to feel guilty...*
> *For forgetting to feel guilty."*
> **Tessa Shafter**

The shock was unimaginable. It shook me to the core, so deep that it truly affected every fibre of my being. I went from a happy, carefree child one minute to being filled with the most complete terror the next. It is so hard to describe in words the rush of emotions that instantly filled my body from my head to my toes. The terror filled every part of me and ran through my veins, carrying it through every part of me. The shock totally immobilized my body and my brain. Everything shut down except for the pain ripping through me at such speed and with such intensity that I couldn't even fully comprehend what I was feeling. That is the initial feeling of shock, and that feeling hung on for days. I think the adrenaline is what makes a person physically capable of being able to get through those early days.

The aftershock came later, after we returned from the funeral and life was supposed to get back to some sort of normal. That was when the next shock wave hit. As we walked through the house, everything I saw only reminded me of what we had lost. The chair at the dining room table that would remain empty, the toothbrush in the bathroom that would never get used, the boots in the woodshed that would never be worn, the toys in the toy box that belonged to him, the bedroom he shared with my baby brother, the marbles and jacks he shared with me...something in every nook and cranny of every room in the house. The terror was still there, but now in a deep, grieving way that I could not shake. This shock made me heavy in body and soul. It followed me everywhere I went, in every thought I had. This shock was unforgiving, never letting me escape the dread, not even for a second. It took over my body completely, holding me tight, restricting even my own breath. Day by day it became a part of me; it made itself at home in my body and would stay with me forever.

As time passed, I became used to this feeling and so adjusted to make room for this new part of me. Eventually, I no longer realized it was there. Little by little, day by day, as the world around me changed, so did I. It happened so slowly that I didn't even realize it was happening. It was happening though, to each one of us, kids and parents. Grief had filled our home and our hearts. The sadness was unbearable, but it was everywhere. There was nowhere to hide. It was like living in a shadowy darkness of our previous lives. It was hard to be home where there were so many reminders, but it was even worse to be away from where he still belonged...the only place he would ever belong again.

It was weird to be with other people. We were definitely the elephant in the room. I could tell that people were awkward around me. People felt as though they should say something, but didn't know what to say so tried to avoid being near me. Then there were those that would try to say some kind or empathetic words, but that was also strange and awkward, and often the words were not helpful. It was not only awkward for them, but for me too. Sometimes a person would ask how I was doing, but they were just hoping to hear that I was okay, and doing fine. That way they could feel good that they had asked, and could move on away from me and from the awkwardness of the situation. Eventually people quit asking, and assumed that because I looked fine I was fine, and had dealt with it and moved on.

No matter how many years pass, people don't get over the loss of a loved one, especially when it is a child that has passed away. I carried on, we all did; we each put on a brave face, continued to live, do normal things, but none of us ever got over the loss. Please join the *Happiness To Healing Closed Facebook Group*, a place where like-minded people can go to gain support, information, and friendship with others that have suffered the loss of a loved one.

After the shock, fear moves in. Fear comes in many shapes, sizes and forms, and is very hard to spot. It comes in small doses, but once fear takes hold in one area, it opens the door for many more fears to enter. Fear of being alone, fear of the dark, fear of waking up, fear of falling asleep, fear of being in public, fear of change, and really a fear of both living and dying, even fears of fear. Again, because fear takes over little by little, I didn't realize I was living in fear. Children are natural risk takers until they learn that fear can keep you safe. I learned this lesson at a very young age. I have never been a risky person. I have always evaluated the risk before doing anything. I have also always been an old soul, a caretaker of sorts. I always thought of this as responsible, not as fearful. I was, even from a young age, a mother hen. As a teenager I was often the mother of the group, checking in with people, making sure everyone was where they should be. I was often the driver so that I could ensure that everyone made it home safe and sound.

Control is simply another form of fear, and anyone who knows me at all knows I like to be in control of every situation, to guide others, watch over them, and always keep them safe. I really just thought this was my nature. My motto has always been "Better safe than sorry." I never stopped to think about why control was so important to me, or how it affected other people or my relationship with them. I was often seen as bossy and snobby, but this never really bothered me. Once people got to know me they realized I wasn't a snob, but most people still thought of me as a bossy person. My "snobbiness" was really just my way of weeding through people. If they assumed I was a snob and didn't want to take the time to get to know me, it was an easy way for me to rid myself of the majority of people that came into my life. The people that cared enough to get to know me were worth the effort to love inside my circle of protection where my personal walls were somewhat lower. Again, fear was doing its job, protecting me from potential hurt.

To this day, I don't have a lot of friends. I need to keep my circle small, to control the number of people who can affect my life, so that I can continue to be as safe as possible. I know this may sound strange, to close myself off from people, but for me it means sanity. A lot of people want outside support when they go through difficult times in life, but to me that meant opening up and then I would have to admit my deepest secrets and fears. I held such deep-seated fear, that if I let it come to the surface I think it would have broken me. So I kept control, and kept my feelings and my fears locked away. Over time, I associated these actions with strength. I liked being capable, of knowing what to do, being independent, knowing that I could take care of myself, and feeling as though I didn't need anyone to take care of me.

However, 43 years later, I now see that these characteristics have affected my relationships, even with my husband. Always being independent and capable doesn't leave a lot of room for being supported. I can clearly see that I also transferred my fears onto my children. While I have managed to keep them safe, I have also kept them from being carefree, adventurous, and have greatly limited their life experiences, and therefore their right to be joyful.

Heartbreak is the perfect word, as my heart literally broke. There was such a huge break that it seemed to be totally unrepairable. The division is strong and deep. The first time a heart breaks is the hardest in many ways, because it is foreign and one has never experienced it before. It hits much harder – like a brick wall. The physical intensity is much greater; sort of like a first pregnancy where the body doesn't recognize what's happening so the feelings are more intense than in following pregnancies. Subsequent heartbreak is every bit as ferocious, but the physical body can relate to the feelings because it has been there before. The body and mind knows it will survive, and this is the cruel part of this heartbreak. Emotionally and mentally you may feel as though you don't want to or won't be able to carry on, but you know with certainty that you will, but that it will be painful, and that the pain and loss will be with you always. The first time you are filled with the fear of the unknown, but each subsequent loss fills you with the heavy dread of the known; the all too familiar knowing that you will continue to exist in a world that you will find very hard to be a part of.

The world around you will go on as usual. People tend to allow a certain time period for grieving, and when you are not "better" by that time, they feel a need to "fix" you or find someone who can. The people in your world want you to be okay so that they can move on in life and not feel guilty that you are stuck or being left behind. This seems to be human nature, and I don't believe this is done to rush or hurt you. I believe that when people are ready to move on, they assume that you should also be ready for the next step. It is also hard for the people around you to see you in pain, and this is simply their way of trying to pull you back from your sorrow. What these people don't understand is that we will all grieve in our own way, in our own time. It is also going to depend on the depth of the relationship between you and the one you have lost, how deeply you will be affected. In my case, after losing a brother, the loss of a grandparent was not nearly as significant, and therefore much easier to handle emotionally. Our own lives and our own experiences, and the emotions and beliefs we each attach to those experiences, will determine greatly how we feel in and move through grief. No one grieves the same way, for the same time period, following the same set of rules, as we are each unique in our values, beliefs and experiences. The kindest thing you can do to support someone through grief is to simply be there when they need you; not when you need them, not when you have time, but to be available for them when they reach out to you.

"People don't always need advice.
Sometimes all they really need is
A hand to hold, an ear to listen,
And a heart to understand them"
Unknown

If you have not yet checked out the Facebook group, please join the Happiness To Healing Closed Facebook Group, a place where like-minded people can go to gain support, information, and friendship with others that have suffered the loss of a loved one.

Chapter Two

Heart Wrenching Sorrow

The news is hard as it makes everything final. It takes away the hope you had and makes death a reality. I knew my brother had been hit by a car, I knew that he had been seriously injured; I knew things were very serious, but I had hope that he would be okay. I prayed very hard that he would be okay.

Again, I cannot recall that timelines of receiving the news. I know my parents returned home from the hospital and gathered us together, and told us that David had died. Again, luckily I understood what death meant , so I was able to grasp what I was being told. I knew death was a forever thing, and that we were not going to get David back. All I really remember, though, is hearing the words. I can't recall where we were, who actually said the words, or what took place next, but I can still feel the heaviness that settled over me.

On June 16, 2000 my nephew Wade was taken from his family at age 12. He was on a school trip with his grade seven class, a class of 13 children. They had taken a glass bottomed boat to Flower Pot Island and had been camping for a few days. They were scheduled to return to Tobermory but the weather turned bad. The captain and the school teachers decided to return even though weather reports were not good. Just fifteen minutes into the return trip the True North II sank deep. My nephew and another young girl never made it back to shore. The other 16 passengers, including 11 students, 1 university student chaperone, 2 extra passengers, 2 teachers and the captain all made it back to the safety of the island shore. Wade and his classmate were missing for another 6 hours. Police divers finally found their bodies the morning of June 17, 2000. Our family had been hopeful again; we had prayed, we had bargained with God, but the news came again. Wade's body had been found, but it was too late!

Two years later my youngest daughter's friend, Bodyne Hutchison also passed away. He had been diagnosed with a brain tumour. They had spent months together, visiting every day after school and on weekends. They had grown very close and enjoyed spending time together. My daughter never seemed to notice that her friend was sick. They played, and laughed, and hugged often. They celebrated holidays together, although sometimes the celebrations were early, as we never knew how much time he had. He had good days and bad days with his illness, but they made the most of each moment they spent together. But then one day, his mom let Jerica know that this day would be her last day to visit her friend because her son didn't want Jerica to remember him the way he was now. He wanted her to think of him the way he used to be. This was so sad; Jerica was heartbroken, but as a mother, I understood that his mom had to do

this for him, and I certainly respected their wishes. Two days later...
we received the news. Her very special friend had passed away, at
age 7. This was also the year of Jerica's First Communion, and she had
a beautiful, long, white gown for the event. During their "dates" they
had talked to each other about love, and how they loved each other.
My daughter's concern after her friend's death was about the future.
She needed to know what would happen if her friend fell in love with
someone else while he was in heaven and she was still on earth; or
what would happen if she fell in love on earth while he was in heaven.
Or what would happen if she fell in love again when she grew up. She
wanted to know that he would still love her, and that he would know
that she would always love him. She wanted him to be happy, and
she needed an answer about how things would work and how they
would find each other in heaven when she got there. His mom set up
a meeting for my daughter to talk to the minister, and he was able to
answer her questions in a way that made sense for a 7 year old. I am
eternally grateful for his words of wisdom to her at that time, as it has
allowed her to grow up and fall in love again.

This news came after they had been able to share a lot of special
time and love together. They both knew that he was sick, and that
there time together was limited, even though they never spoke about
that. They were at peace and love with one another, and each knew
how greatly they were loved by the other. For this too, I am grateful,
but the news no less was very painful to hear. The news no less is
final. The news no less breaks our hearts, and changes us forever.

Helen Murray

**"Love is the hardest drug to quit, but
It is even harder when it is taken away."**
Unknown

My world has taught me many lessons. Some I learned earlier than most and some have taken me an entire lifetime to figure out. I have learned that I am a survivor, and I have learned that I no longer just want to survive. I have learned that life is too short for some, and too long for others. I have learned that love is the strongest emotion of all, but that anger can engulf you. Love can break you, and heal you if you let it. Anger can get you through the toughest of times, but keep you from the best life has to offer. I have seen with my own eyes how deep sadness can pull a person down, and how difficult it can be to escape its grip. I have learned that burying your emotional trauma can create illness, and keep you suffering mentally, physically, and emotionally, but just recently I have also learned that your emotions can also free you!

I have seen that fear can keep you from living your life to its fullest, but it can keep you safe at times. Fear can cause sickness, it can keep you from taking risks, it can turn into perfectionism and indecisiveness, and it can create a lack of trust, of confidence and self-worth. Fear can blind you, make you bitter, and even become hatred; it can take away your courage and your power. It can completely debilitate your mind, body and soul. I have also learned that all we have to fear is fear itself.

However, we can also choose not to be fearful. We can choose to face our fears, and challenge them. We can take control, accept them for what they are, acknowledge them, thank them, and then let them go. Your fears are nothing more than thoughts in your head. They may come from your beliefs, but they are yours, and you can choose to hold on to them and continue to feel fearful, or you can choose to recognize them, eliminate them, and set yourself free. This may seem strange to you right now, but it is true. You can change your fear, use it as motivation, and not continue to be debilitated by its power over you.

It won't happen overnight, it won't happen all at once, but with guidance, support and practice you can put your fears to rest. Sometimes these feelings and beliefs have been with you for so long, and are so deeply embedded in your subconscious mind, that you forget you have the power to allow or deny them into your daily life. For many, many years, every time I heard an ambulance siren, I had an internal feeling of panic. I instantly became still and did a silent role call of all of my loved ones. Where were each of them driving, would they be on this road at this time of day, what time of day would they be driving, could it be in the direction the ambulance was heading, and on and on with the excruciating questions until I was finally through the complete list of possibilities. Then I would spend the remainder of my day feeling ill, stressed and completely out of sorts until I knew each and every one of them was home safe and sound. We live on a busy highway with a lot of ambulance traffic, as we are in between two towns with hospitals. My husband and one daughter work shift work, and the others all travel to and from work and school. This anxiety would wash over me several times a day, and could be 24/7 because of the various shifts my family was working. When my children were young we NEVER travelled on long weekends – EVER! I can't stand to be in traffic, and there are always so many deaths on long weekends. Of course, as the kids got older and were able to make their own decisions they would go away with friends for long weekends. I was a nervous wreck from the time they would leave until they finally returned home from the weekend. I did my best to encourage them to be safe and have fun, but I always felt sick as they drove away. Luckily, they all knew how hard it was for me so they would all text me when they arrived and again when they were heading out on the return trip. At least this way I could remain somewhat calm for an appropriate length of time, and I tried my best to factor extra time into their travels for heavy traffic, or stopping to eat. If they were past what I had allowed to be a reasonable time the panic would set in and I would be sick until they arrived home. I did my very best not to text them, and I was usually successful with that because I could never allow myself to text in case they would answer me while they were driving, because then I would just have another worry in my head. So you can see how these thoughts can take over and create havoc in your daily life so easily. I lived this way for years and never even stopped to think that there could be another option. My mind was running on auto pilot, and I was letting fear control me. My own thoughts were keeping me from enjoying my own life, and even worse I had passed those beliefs onto my children. I was keeping them from knowing true happiness and joy, as I had filled them with fear as well.

> *"You can clutch the past so tightly*
> *To your chest that it leaves your*
> *Arms too full to embrace the present"*
> **Jane Glidewell**

This quote says it so well. I was holding on to past fears so intensely that there was no possible way I could ever be fully present in the here and now. Even my love for my children was tainted by the fear I held so close. I was so blind to my beliefs that I was unable to see what I was missing today...everyday!

> *"Death is not the greatest loss in life.*
> *The greatest loss is what dies inside*
> *Us while we live"*
> **Norman Cousins**

Loss, no matter how it occurs, is a deep grief like no other. A sudden loss causes your body to go into shock, but with illness that shock hits you when you first learn of the illness and prognosis of the disease. One type of death is no easier or less painful than another. Emotions are just simply spread over time with an illness, whereas a sudden death engulfs you with all of the emotions at once. *I am offering a free 15 minute private Discovery Session, one on one, with me if you are interested in learning how to heal your way to happiness. Go to www.ijustwanttobehappybook.com to get your free session.*

For me, the hardest loss is for a parent to lose a child. My heart goes out to parents who have suffered this tragedy and pain. I can only imagine the depths of their sorrow as I know the pain I have felt at losing a brother and a nephew, and watching my children suffer the pain and sorrow of losing their young cousin and friends. My family lives in a very small community of about 2000 people, and our community has been affected with the tragedy of child loss too many times.

Now that my children are grown, they tease me about how protective I was as a parent. I would let them ride their bikes in our circle driveway, but only with helmets, knee pads, and elbow pads. They were never allowed to ride on the road. We live on a dead end road with less than a dozen houses on it, all on the same side of the street. The kids were not permitted to walk into town unless they were with either my husband or me, until they turned 16. If they wanted to go roller blading, I loaded them all up into the minivan and drove them to the school parking lot, dressed them in all of their protective gear, and they were able to skate there while I watched. Then I would load them all up again, and drive them home. Even as young adults, if they went out I would make countless trips to ensure they and all of their friends had a safe ride home. One night, I made

7 trips. There was a RIDE program in town, and I was wearing my pajamas since it was late and I had already been in bed. On my seventh pass through the RIDE program the police officer asked what I was doing, and if I would be done for the night anytime soon as she was tired of seeing me so many times in one night. I assured her that this was my last trip as I had picked up the last of the kids needing a ride. I think she thought I was a bit ridiculous, but I always told my kids that I would come at any hour of the day or night, and would make as many trips as was needed. You can't tell your kids this if you don't mean it.

At one point, our home was broken into. My husband insisted that we start locking our doors at night and when no one was home. I did it for a little bit, but I felt very uneasy about it. I was terrified that someone would need to get into the house for safety and find a locked door. Eventually we agreed to change the lock system over to a keyless entry system so that all of the kids and their friends could get in the house no matter what time of day or night it was. I just couldn't sleep knowing that I had potentially locked someone out, and away from safety. Loss changes the way you think. It creates fear and insecurity within you. It lurks in the background, even when you are not consciously aware of it. It teaches you to always be alert for danger, to evaluate risk at every moment, and to play it safe. Thankfully my children were able to realize that I acted this way out of love, and respected my needs as well as their own. They always let me know where they were, who they were with, what they were doing and when they would be home or where they would be staying. They are now aged 22, 24, 26, and 27 and continue to do this for me out of love. Even though there were times I drove them all crazy, they have always understood my need to know they are safe. For this, I thank them all from the bottom of my heart. I know many parents have many worrisome nights wondering where their children are. My heart goes out to all parents; it is not an easy job!

My life became quiet after my brother's death. My mom slept a lot, and suffered very bad headaches. It was important that she be able to rest while the house was quiet so she could manage to make it through the times of noise and busyness. I was very close with my mom as we spent a lot of time together, just the two of us. I think even at a young age I was intuitive to her needs. Being "good" was necessary in the early years, and it wasn't difficult for me to be good. My older siblings were in school and my younger brother was only a baby, so I was used to being and playing alone and finding ways to entertain myself. Some children are just naturally easy children and I was one of them. I would make up quiet games that I could play next to my mom that would only require minimal participation from her. One of my favourite games was to pretend I was buying things and paying by cheque. I would use the empty carbon copy from her cheque book and buy all kinds of interesting things, and then get her to sign the cheque. I was aware that children were not able to sign cheques. She would sign with an X because it was all she could manage some days, as her head often hurt too much for her to lift it off the pillow. I questioned the validity of signing a cheque with an X, and she explained to me that it is allowed as a legal signature if people were unable to spell or write their own names. A "mark" is valid in place of a written signature. This is a funny tidbit of information for a 5 year old child to hold onto, but for some reason this has always remained a vivid memory for me. It is also strange that so much of those early years are a blur for me, but the memories I do have are very strong, vivid, concrete memories.

Being good, being quiet, became a way of life for me. I actually enjoyed the calmness of this, and still do to this day. I spent a lot of time playing with my dolls as well, often outside in the sunshine in our back yard. I would spend time creating the environment, and setting up the story as well as getting everything prepared and just right. Sometimes it was difficult when everyone returned home, and the house became noisy and chaotic again. The days were peaceful, and then suddenly people were there giving orders and asking questions, and bossing me around. I think my mom also had difficulty with this, and when she got overtired or overwhelmed she would faint. My dad would pick her up and carry her to the couch and get her covered up and settled in. Then the house would need to quiet down again so she could rest. Now as a coach, I find this to be so interesting because fainting is the physical reaction to fear, and not being able to cope. Looking back I can see that this is exactly what was happening to my mom; when things got to the point of overwhelm for her, her body simply checked out. Interestingly enough, I began fainting when I was about 18 years old, in my second year of college. I had all sorts of testing done, and it was discovered that I had very low blood pressure and some sort of issue in the back of my neck that if I tipped my neck at the wrong angle it would make me faint. No one could really explain what was causing the fainting spells. Again, looking back it makes total sense. I had learned that fainting is the cure for overwhelm, so when life became stressful, my body kicked in to protect me and just shut everything down.

So, in short, I enjoyed "being good" and it became part of who I was for a very long time. My mom would sometimes ask me "Are you behaving?" and I would respond "I am being haved." She even found a t-shirt that had a picture of a princess and the words "I Am Miss Behaving" which became one of my all-time favourite shirts. I enjoyed being good, and I liked helping my mom. I think this is part of the reason I have now become a life coach; I am passionate about helping people become the best "you" you can be!

As you will become aware, unfortunately, I was not always able to remain this "good" person, but it has always been with me, and in me underneath all of the other parts of me that would come into being. This is the part of me that I lost along the way, but desperately wanted to get back; the person who is happiest in the quiet solitude, the person who truly is inspired by helping others, and the one who is still inspired by that little girl from the past. I am on a journey to find inner peace, happiness, gratitude, forgiveness, and true joy. It's been too many years. Life is only as hard as we make it, and change is only one decision away. If you are looking for positive changes in your life go to www.ijustwanttobehappybook.com and click on "are-you-ready-for-change" article to download your free PDF.

This new feeling came when I started school. Thankfully, back then, it was only every other day Kindergarten. I didn't want to go to school; there was no part of me that thought this was going to be fun or exciting. My mom had made a new outfit for me to wear my first day, a seersucker pants and shirt set. It was my favorite colour, red, and I loved my new clothes. But...when I had to leave for school that first day, the thought of having to ride the school bus and leave the safety of our home was overwhelming. As I walked down the sidewalk and stepped onto the gravel laneway the fear was too much. I threw myself into a huge mud puddle on the laneway. I was soaked and muddy, my hair was a mess and I had ruined my new clothes! But there I lay; I had found a way out...or so I thought. My mom picked me up, took me back into the house, and my sisters made their way down the lane to wait for the school bus. I changed out of my wet clothes, had a bath, and got dressed again in fresh clothing. My dad came home, and drove me to school in my own yellow bus. My dad at that time drove an old-fashioned style yellow pickup truck. In previous years he had driven me to the babysitter's in this pickup and he always joked that I had my very own special school bus.

27

I made friends and played with other kids, but was always happiest when at home. At school no one really cares the same. Everyone has to do certain things at certain times. Everyone is expected to just do as you are told whether you like it or not. School is also very noisy; very different than the quiet solitude I had become used to. My teacher was very nice, and I actually liked her very much. I know I was old for my age; I was not your typical 5 year old, and I felt disconnected from the school world. I was much more used to an adult world where things were quieter and more civilized, and conversation was more meaningful. At least Kindergarten was in a small one-room school house, and not an entire school. This was a comfort as the big school seemed quite intimidating to me when we would go there for something for my sisters. School was not an intimate place where I felt safe and relaxed; it remained a place that never quite fit me, a place where you are one of many, and no one was made to feel welcome or special.

I went through school never excelling, but always managing. School was uneventful for the most part – something you had to do, so it was done. So it went until high school. People seemed to be mulling about everywhere and at most it seemed without any sense of purpose. Teachers taught one way, and it was just too darn bad if that didn't work for you. People were rude, mean and hurtful to one another. Teachers were often the worst offenders of this behavior. I realized very quickly that this was not the place for me. I didn't do well in high school by any means. Looking back now, I know this was due to my own mindset and the choices I made, but I think if I was put in that same situation again today, it would probably have much the same final outcome. I was often outraged by the way teachers treated students, and that students seemed to have no idea that they could stand up for themselves regarding the injustices being put upon them. I spent a lot of time in the principal's office, not because I was sent there, but because I chose to go there and make a point of the behavior that was commonplace in classrooms. I somehow felt that it was my duty to stand up for other students and challenge the teacher's inappropriate and unprofessional behavior. I myself was rarely the subject of this mistreatment, but I refused to sit and watch other students be treated in such ways. This is when I found my own voice. It may have been easier for me to sit and pretend that I didn't notice the injustices, and perhaps in the end it would have been the smarter choice, but at that time in my life, for whatever reason, I was compelled to be the voice for those who could not speak up for themselves. Teachers degraded students emotionally, badgered them verbally, and at times were even physically abusive. We had a grade 10 geography teacher who loved to show his strength and power over students, and on more than one occasion threw students down the staircase. Once he battled with a student and ended up throwing him out of the plate glass window from the second storey onto the sidewalk below. One day while in his class I was chewing gum; yes, chewing gum was against the rules. He told me to put the gum on the tip of my nose. I refused, but did get up and throw it in the garbage. Apparently this outraged him. He became furious with me, and told me to get it out of the trash and put it on my nose. Again, I refused, at which point he grabbed me and dragged me out into the hallway landing at the top of the staircase. He yelled that I could either put the gum on my nose or he would throw me down the stairs. Again, I refused and said if he chose to throw me down the stairs I would be sure to make sure he went down with me. There were many classrooms off this hallway, and by now I had engaged in a very loud battle of wills with him, but not one classroom door opened. Not one teacher even poked their head out of their room to see what was going on, not one student left the safety of their seats. This still astounds me. In a school of more than 500 people, not one person chose to help another human being. The teacher did let go of me and did not try to throw me down the stairs, but this was the day that I knew for sure that school was not for me. I ended up quitting high school before the end of my Grade 10 year. I have no regrets about my decision, but that moment in time also changed my life.

Chapter 3

Faith

I have found that it is very easy to feel confused when you have suffered loss. I saw this more for my own children than for myself. Each of my children reacted so differently to their loss, even though it was the same loss. I never thought of this when it was my parents dealing with us. It's difficult to know how and what to do for each child. When my nephew was missing I gathered my children together and broke the news to them calmly and clearly, with the information I had at that point in time. I let them each react in their own way while trying my best to love and console each one of them. We discussed what we could do together to help each other while we waited for more news. We decided that we would read a bible story but no one could pick which story, so we decided that when I opened the book, whichever story it opened to we would read. I sat in the arm chair and they all climbed up and squeezed in together. The book opened to the story of Jesus walking on water. This story infuriated my oldest daughter, but gave my second oldest immense peace. While one child saw this as stupid because if Jesus was really walking on water he could have just reached down through the water and saved Wade, the other saw this story as Wade not being alone and scared because

Jesus was with him. The two younger kids, age 5 and 7, didn't really express their opinions of the story or the subsequent discussions of the story and its meaning. This was a very long night. I had quit smoking three months earlier, but that night I went to the store and bought a pack of smokes. My husband worked long hours, and had an hour and a half commute each way. I had finally managed to track him down; he was a truck driver and delivered ice cream and yogurt to stores in the GTA, Greater Toronto Area. Neither of us had cell phones then. He got home as quickly as he could. I had managed to somehow keep myself together until the moment I saw him, and then I started sobbing. I couldn't hold back the tears. He was my strength and support that day. He just held me while I cried my heart out. I will never forget that moment, and how much I appreciated him for letting me cry and not having to be strong.

My husband was shaken that day as well. Parents are incredible people, though, in their love for their children. It still amazes me how strong parents can be when their children need them. He held himself strong until we were back home after all the funeral proceedings and family gatherings were over. He opened his father's day gift when he returned home. The kids had gotten him some stepping stones to make a path from the driveway to the deck. Each stone had a verse on it, and this was his undoing. He opened his gift, thanked the kids and left the room in tears. Sixteen years later the stones are still in the attic and have never been laid in the ground. We re-did the deck this summer and I think we are finally ready to put the garden stones on the path.

My kids all have different feelings about Church, God and spirituality. In the end, I let them chose their own path. This wasn't always easy for me to do, but you cannot force people to make the same choices you make, and unconditional love is about supporting each other no matter what. They all have different thoughts about spirituality, but they are all good people who care deeply about others. My point here is that we will all react differently based on our own past experiences. We will all grieve in our own way; we will all follow a different path to healing. It's okay. We are all right where we are supposed to be, doing exactly what we are supposed to be doing. Sometimes we have different lessons to learn, which may take us down several paths before we get it all figured out. Be kind and patient with yourself! It's okay to be who you are.

I was raised Catholic, but my mother always said there was some Presbyterian mixed in too. My dad's family were staunch Catholics, my mother's family was Presbyterian and we were somewhere in between. My mother did become a Catholic when my parents were married. We went to church every Sunday, sang in the choir, cleaned the church, my mom belonged to the CWL, and we had Sunday school classes all summer long. There was no Catholic school in Drayton so we went to public school. This meant, however, that we had our catechism classes in the summer months. The nuns ran the classes and they were full-day classes.

All in all we were a religious family, but not staunch Catholics. First Communion takes place in the spring of Grade two. There are classes leading up to the actual ceremony. I loved these classes; for some reason I found peace during this time. I asked my parents to create a prayer station for me at home. They brought a small wooden bookcase upstairs and placed it just outside of our bedroom door. There were four of us sharing a bedroom, so space in there was at a premium. It was perfect in the hallway as it was private and a place all my own. The shelf was short enough that I could kneel to say my prayers and rest my arms on the top of the case. I insisted on having my own holy water so I could bless myself during my prayers. My mother diligently brought me home a fresh jar of holy water each week from church. I had prayer cards, prayer books, bible story books, my mother's bible (Presbyterian version) all set up in my prayer station. Each morning when I awoke, and each night before bed I knelt and said my prayers.

Looking back, this was probably a strange request from a 7 year old, but it was what I needed at the time, and my parents provided it without question. My prayer station stayed in the hallway until we moved, when I was 11. I never set it up in our new house, even though I now had my own space. I know for sure though that it was this prayer station that helped develop my deep sense of faith. I also find it strange that I have always called it "faith." I am a person of great faith, but I would not say that I am terribly religious, at least by most religious people's standards. I believe in God, but I don't care if you follow a certain religion, or if you are spiritual, faithful, have belief in a higher power, the Universe, Buddha...whatever you choose. I do hope with all my heart that every person can believe in something bigger than themselves, some higher power.

My faith has been challenged on more than one occasion in my life. There was a time I left religion and felt as though my faith had wavered. I no longer go to church on a regular basis, and haven't now for about 9 years. Even as a child I would argue with my mom, that Jesus and God were not just found at church. She said going to church was important, and I said you don't need to be in a church to believe in God. I still believe strongly that it is our actions every day that show we are good people, not only while sitting in church. There are people who go to church often that are not filled with faith, and there are people who are filled with faith and it has nothing to do with church or religion. Again, for me, it is not about who you choose to believe in, but simply that you choose to believe. When I look back at all the events in my life I know that I could not have managed without my faith to hold onto and carry me through.

My faith was challenged during my fourth pregnancy. We were 17 weeks along and had our first ultrasound. It had been a very easy pregnancy to this point. Of course by the fourth you feel like an old pro. I hadn't had any morning sickness, and was healthy, active and things were going smoothly. I arrived on time to the appointment, feeling somewhat uncomfortable due to all the water I had to drink. We lived in Arthur but still doctored in Brampton as I was very happy with our doctor and she had delivered all of our children. Our drive was about an hour and a half so the doctor was always kind and set tests and appointments on the same day to save me driving with three young children. After the ultrasound we had lunch and then went on to our doctor's appointment. The ultrasound results were back so we were able to get it all taken care of in one day. When we met with the doctor she explained that the ultrasound was showing five cysts on the baby's brain. She told us that we would need monthly ultrasounds from now on, and then in the last month we would need weekly ultrasounds so they could continue to monitor the cysts closely. She then explained that these cysts were a strong indicator of Trisomy 18, also known as Edwards Syndrome. We were booked into genetic counselling immediately. During this counselling we were told that the baby would most likely be born with Trisomy 18, but that we should have an amniocentesis to know better. However, I was now considered to be a high risk pregnancy and an amniocentesis was also a risk. They further explained that if the baby was born with Trisomy 18 she would have a two month life expectancy and would be completely mentally and physically disabled.

We were to go home, discuss it together, and make a decision. I felt the risk of the amnio was too great, and didn't really see why they would suggest putting a baby through more risk. The next week when we returned for another counselling session I questioned this thinking. I guess the shock of everything we heard that first day had been enough to take in. So they explained that the amnio would give us a much better chance of knowing if the baby did indeed have Trisomy 18, but we would not know for sure. I guess I was a bit dense because I still couldn't understand why anyone would want to create more risk for the baby. Finally, it was explained that after the amniocentesis results came back we could make an educated decision on whether or not to end the pregnancy. I was stunned!   I couldn't believe what I was hearing. There was no way in hell that I would abort my baby. I let them know that abortion was not an option. They booked us in for continued counselling. No one told me that I could decline these sessions. By the time a month had gone by and I had my next doctor's appointment, I was very frustrated. My husband was having a difficult time and just wasn't sure that he could handle having a baby that was going to be severely handicapped and would only live for two months. My heart broke for him, but I knew that I could never kill my own child. I also believed that that if this was the baby God gave us then this was the baby we would have and love for as long as we had it with us. We discussed it with the doctor, and she said that legally she had to send us for counselling to ensure that we knew all of our rights, but that we could choose to stop going at any time. We cancelled the next appointments. My husband agreed, and I assured him that that we were going to be okay and that we were strong enough to handle whatever happened. The rest of the pregnancy was stressful for my husband, but for me a very calm, peacefulness blanketed me for the remainder of the pregnancy.

> ***"If we deny love that is given to us,***
> ***if we refuse to give love because of***
> ***fear, pain or loss, then our lives will***
> ***be empty, our loss greater"***
> **Anonymous**

February 3, 1994 I received my own precious miracle. I had three false labours; got to the hospital three times only to have the labour stop. The third time I decided I wasn't leaving – I was having a baby. My doctor agreed to break my water and get things going. She and I both knew that as soon as my water broke things would move quite quickly. My nurse came into the room and said she was going on break and would be back in 15 minutes to check on me. I let her know that in about 20 minutes everything would be over and done and we would have a baby. She kind of chuckled and left the room. I suppose she didn't know that this was my fourth, or that it was a high risk pregnancy, but at the time I wasn't really thinking about what she did or didn't know.

My husband and I were left alone in the labour room. Things were moving very quickly, and contractions were coming hard and fast. He went and found the doctor; the nurse had not returned yet. The doctor came back into the room and we were well on our way to delivering the baby when the nurse walked back into the room. My husband and I were very apprehensive as we were uncertain if our baby would be okay. The baby was born – a girl! The first thing I asked the doctor was if she had 10 fingers, 10 toes and does she have Trisomy 18? At this point I realized the baby was not making any noise.

I could see the doctor was concerned, but no one was answering me! It felt like eternity...I couldn't see the baby and no one was talking. Then I heard the doctor speaking quite harshly to the nurse. "Why is the oxygen table not hooked up and ready for use, especially knowing this was a high risk situation?" My head was spinning, my stomach sank. I couldn't see anything! Finally my husband came to the bed and told me that the cord had been wrapped around her neck three times, and they were trying to get her breathing. I felt ill; I needed to see my baby. What was wrong? Why was it taking so long? Seconds seemed to be hours.

Suddenly I heard her cry. My heart was filled with joy at that moment. The doctor said she was breathing normally now and was just wrapping her in a blanket. As she walked towards me with the baby I asked again if she had 10 fingers, 10 toes. I realized at that moment I could not have loved her less no matter what night have been wrong. The doctor answered yes, and said she was absolutely perfect in every way! I finally got to hold her, and as I gazed into her eyes I realized I was gazing upon a miracle. She had no signs of Trisomy 18; she was absolutely amazing.

Chapter 4

Going On

I don't think I really learned how to keep going; it's just something you do. At first you just wake up every morning, and live putting one foot in front of the other. You do the things in life that have to be done like eating, sleeping, going to school and work. You truly are just going through the motions, and mostly because you don't know what else to do. Sometimes this is the cruel part of life; you wake up each morning and put one foot in front of the other whether you want to or not. Time passes slowly, and every action is hard. Many days it seems unfair that you wake up, and you wish with all your heart that you could be with the person you lost so that your heart would stop aching. Each day you become a bit more accustomed to the way you feel, and therefore, each day you are a bit more numb than you were the day before.

Eventually it is five years later and you realize that you didn't think about the hole in your life every minute of every day. Then it is 10 years later and certain days are really hard but other days come and go without thoughts of your loved ones popping into your mind, no matter where you are, who you are with or what you are doing. The problem with just going through the motions and not dealing with them is that over time it becomes a way of life. Feelings just get buried deeper within but they are still there, ready to sabotage at any given moment. Rather than accepting how you feel you ignore your inner voice.

By doing this I was teaching myself not to trust myself. This mistrust soon translates into not trusting others. Once mistrust creeps into your inner self, it becomes habitual. Our subconscious mind remembers all the times we've chosen not to trust our instincts, and if we can't trust ourselves, then our subconscious will jump in to protect us from trusting others. Our subconscious mind really acts like muscle memory. It remembers past events and how we reacted to those events. When our body and mind are replicating those past feelings, it brings up those stored files from our archives and immediately takes over, driving on autopilot, steering us down the road most travelled. Somewhere along the journey we stop making decisions and simply run on auto pilot. When this happens we revert to our natural instinctive behavior of fight, flight or freeze.

These instinctive behaviours may be needed in the immediate time after the loss of a loved one because this instinct is what keeps us going, what makes us get up, and continue to live. However, when it becomes habitual in nature it is not a good thing as it keeps us trapped where we are. It keeps us living in a place of fear, mistrust and primal instinct. *If you are stuck in flight, fight or freeze mode, and are unable to release yourself from your fears, I invite you to a free 15 minute one on one discovery coaching session to uncover what is holding you back from emotional freedom. Simply go to www.ijustwanttobehappybook.com.*

Looking strong is a fantastic way of covering up your own fears and insecurities. The outside world sees someone who has it all together. Hold your head high, keep your shoulders back, walk swiftly, and look like you have a mission. People see these attributes as strength. We have all heard of a phone voice or public face; as with any skill practice makes perfect. The problem is when you practice the skill of not being the authentic you, you will no longer be the authentic you. In essence by hiding your insecurities and your fears you have also hidden yourself. I thought hiding would keep me safe, protect me from further harm, but I guess that really depends on whether you feel it is a safe to lose yourself, to forget yourself or to ignore yourself. I think it is easier, and that is why so many of us do it. If you become disguised then no one will ever be able to hurt you. However, no one will ever be able to truly know you either. You may wake up one day and not even recognize yourself, or at least not your inner self. I think this is what I have done for so many years, that I actually don't know myself. Often the way I see myself and the way other people see me are totally different. I think I'm an impatient person and yet when I was working with a staff of 50 women they considered one of my biggest attributes to be my patience level.

I think being strong is just a way of covering up fear. I took great pride in knowing that I was strong, in knowing that I had the answers, in knowing I knew what to do every step of the way. The sad part of that was by always knowing I missed out on a lot of opportunity to find out who I really was. Hiding shows in the way we speak to one another; hiding shows up in just so many ways in life, not signing your name to things, not having an opinion, not being confident enough to share your opinion, dressing in monochromatic color schemes, anything to keep you from being noticed. A lot of people feel it's just easier to blend into the background. Now for me that wasn't so. I love to have bright colours, I always had an opinion and was more than happy to share it. I liked being the voice of authority but I think for me that was also hiding because as long as I have the voice of authority people don't question that I may be living in fear. So for me it was a way to keep people out. Assuming this authoritative personality was a way for me to keep people at arm's length, and not be questioned or make close friendships. I have a very small inner circle of close friends and outside of that I have acquaintances and co-workers.

I think working and being busy helped me hide even further. As long as I was busy and had something to do, I didn't have to engage with the people around me. I like to be busy, I like to be on the move, and I like doing physical things. I think it was a way for me to hide from myself as well because as long as my body was busy enough my mind didn't have to think. I didn't have to let my subconscious thoughts enter into my conscious mind. It's hard to explain but I think that I modeled myself after my father, from a very young age. He was a very hard worker, a very busy person; nothing was ever too much for him. He always knew the answers, knew what to do, took charge of the situation. He never faltered, he was never weak, and I think in my young years I modelled myself after his behavior. I used to always say that I didn't like emotions, I hated crying, you know crying doesn't give you anything but a runny nose and a headache. I thought that people who showed their emotions were not strong people; basically I thought they should just suck it up and move on. Nothing in life is that bad, and you know once you have suffered the death of a close family member, it is very hard to become emotional about other smaller things. But again, for so many years I trained myself to be like that, and I refused to let myself be emotional for fear that, if the emotions ever started I would not be able to shut them off. For me, being emotional was not a privilege I could afford. I was afraid that if the floodgates opened they would never stop. I was afraid that if I ever had a weak moment, insanity would definitely take over and I would not be able to continue living a normal life day to day. *I have created a "Happiness Handbook" for you to assist you on your personal journey of healing to happiness. Please grab your free copy at www.ijustwanttobehappybook.com.*

For a child as young as five, it's very hard to understand how life can be so dramatically different in the course of a 24 hour period. One day you are healthy, happy and vibrant, and the next day your heart is broken and your whole life has been shattered. I'm not sure that anyone at age 5 can make sense of that, can come to an understanding. But, the cruelty of suffering that kind of heartbreak is that you wake up the next day, and the next day and the next day, and you just continue putting one foot in front of the other. Understanding really doesn't play into it in the beginning. At first you have to understand that your life has changed, your brother is gone, your heart is broken, and you feel nothing like the person you used to be. Everyone around you has changed; your family unit has changed. You do try to grasp some sort of understanding but it is very difficult because all you see around you is sadness. My parents were heartbroken; my siblings were going through the same emotions I was, although we are each different people and we each see every event and react to every event differently. There is some process that happens in your mind and you're grasping for bits of understanding, and then over time you understand that things will be quite different moving forward. You understand your siblings will be different moving forward, you understand your parents are not the same parents they used to be, you understand you are not the person you used to be.

Even the most normal, everyday activities are not the way they used to be. You don't get the same joy from things; you don't see the light and the happiness in the world around you. Yes, there are still times when you're happy and there are still times that are good, but for a long, long time, those happy moments, or light moments, are few and far between. I know I have spoken about animals being a big part of our lives; we always had horses, and that brought everyone in our family a lot of fun times. Even that was no longer the same. Yes, we had to go to the barn, yes we had to do chores, yes we had to brush the ponies, yes we had to feed them, and yes we still loved them, but the joy in doing those activities was gone. It's funny, animals may be the one true friend that you have because they are so instinctive; they just pick up on how you're feeling, and they love you for who you are no matter what. Definitely, animals are therapy for people who are going through a stressful time in their life.

As time continues, you definitely get a different understanding as well. You understand that people outside of your family have moved on, that they are still leading a normal life, they are still having fun, in a way that you just can't even fathom. We were still children, we still went to school, we still played outside, and ran around at recess with our friends, but these were things that we did in a very different way. You don't have the same sparkle or the same shine to you, you still do these things but you don't get the same enjoyment anymore.

Then, as I grew older, I still did teenage things; I would go out with my friends and go to parties. I was outspoken, I ended up quitting high school because I was so outspoken and because I was so outraged by what I saw happening in high school. The way I saw teachers treating students, the way students treated other students, the hierarchy, and the clique-iness. I guess it boils down to the fact that different things matter; the normal everyday childhood, teenage things just don't matter anymore.

Things like love and kindness matter, and don't get me wrong, I was a typical teenager and I wasn't always kind to every person I met. You also become jaded when you hear people talking about things that just don't matter and people spend so much energy on. The clothes they are wearing, the gossip; I just didn't fit in to that world anymore. I was much more comfortable with adults, whose problems to me seemed much more real world, real life problems. And actually, from the time I was very young I was more comfortable with adults than I was with other kids my own age. My mother was always very adamant that we befriend the children in school that had no friends. It was an expectation that we would befriend those kids and have them over to our house on Saturdays because she felt very much that every person needed a friend and that as a human being it is our responsibility to ensure that every person has someone they can call a friend.

So that is how we were raised, and I must say that I raised our children in much the same way. For me, though, it was almost a hypocritical type of kindness. I reserved that kindness for people that I thought deserved it, that were worthy of my friendship. I was definitely being judgmental. The popular people or the cocky people that went around thinking that they were all that and a bag of chips, I did not befriend. Of course this is not being a truly gracious, kind-hearted person. This is judging who I believe needs a friend and who I believe needs empathy, and really that is not what it's all about. It is about being kind and gracious to every person that you meet. It is also about assuming, and to assume that I knew every ones story was arrogant and ignorant to say the least. *Please visit www.ijustwanttobehappybook.com to download your free "the-change-challenge" article which will give you tips on creating lasting, positive change in your life.*

I have changed over the years, slowly but surely, day by day. I was very precocious as a young child. I was old beyond my years; however, after my brother's death I started to change. I saw this again when my nephew died and my children's heart broke for the first time; I had to watch them start to change day by day as well. It's very sad that adults don't understand how deeply children are affected by death. I have heard so many adults say "Oh, they're kids, they'll bounce back quickly. You know they really don't internalize this; they are so young they just won't remember." These are always words spoken from an adult who has not suffered the loss of a close family member or friend at a very young age. Anyone who has suffered that kind of trauma understands completely how people will change. We are no longer on the path to being the people we were intended to be, or living the life we were intended to live.

I remember often saying to my mom when I was young that the stork dropped me at the wrong house. I was sure I was destined to be wealthy, . Mom would laugh. I was a precocious child; I was the fifth child, I was very close to my dad, and he definitely treated me like a little princess. Every day he curled my hair into ringlets on his finger, and he tied the bows on the back of my dress. From a very young age I knew my life was meant to be different. We were not a well off family. My parents were both very young when they got married, had very limited education and they certainly worked hard and provided for their family to the best of their ability but we were not a wealthy family, a blue collar family. And yet from a young age I knew that wasn't what was meant for my life. I just had this knowing that I was meant to be wealthy.. However, here I am, almost 45 years later, and I still have this same feeling that I was meant to have a very different life, that I was destined to be wealthy and I was destined to do something more with my life. But it just goes to show you that if you are not determined to make those changes in your life they won't happen for you.

My brother passed away when I was five, and my life went down a different path from that day forward. I became very closed off to the world. I had a make-believe friend and for many years I did not realize that she was not real person. It wasn't until many years later when I asked my mom about her, and my mom told me she wasn't real, and yet she was probably the most real person in my life for about a five year time span. I did not understand that I was changing; it happened so slowly that I did not recognize the changes. However, over the years I adopted what I call the "smile and nod." It was the easiest way to be in a crowd and not really have to engage. When people spoke to me I nodded my head and smiled. It's just easier to live and to make it through your day not exposing yourself to the outside world. I know for certain that I fell in love with my husband because he was strong enough to let me be the way I was, be the person I was, and not try to change me. He accepted me for who I was and he liked who I was. I didn't intimidate him, whereas most guys found me intimidating. He just ignored all of the vibes I put out to the universe and loved me anyways. I've often said that he may not be the perfect husband, but he is absolutely 100% the perfect husband for me. He just gets me! But we do change, and it is sort of like a butterfly in the cocoon. Butterflies spend months in the cocoon getting ready to live their life as a butterfly, but if someone tampers with their cocoon, they will not develop as they should and will end up living a different life than they were headed for. I think for me the biggest thing was that I totally blocked my emotions from a very young age. I saw from a very young age that people wanted to know that everybody was ok, and if you weren't ok they were very uncomfortable around you. So to be able to go out into the world you had to put on a brave face that would show people you were ok, and when people asked you how you were doing you had to be able to say that everything was fine and that you were doing ok. I can't pinpoint when that happened, or if there was a particular incident. I think it was more a day-to-day reinforcement of the way I should behave. To

the external world I seemed like a very confident person, and that's
the way I liked it.

Chapter 5

Becoming Distant

The simple meaning of shut down is the act of stopping the operation or activity; so, in other words, to disengage. While the day-to-day activities of life continue on, and you continue to participate, it is in a disengaged manner. You participate physically, but you don't engage emotionally. In the beginning, I feel this is simply because you are unable to be fully present emotionally. Once you have suffered an emotional trauma, you are just not capable of truly being present for all the mundane activities that continue in your life because you are still consumed mind, body and soul in the grief.

As time passes, though, this disengagement becomes habitual. You start to learn that you can appear to be present and even interact without fully being present in the moment. I learned that I could participate on the outside with my conscious mind, without having to fully engage with those around me. I also learned that many people are also happy then, because as long as you are there, interacting normally, it is much easier for those people to be around you. Life becomes easier this way, for you, and for those around you.

As I said in the previous chapter, I created an imaginary friend. This friend listened to me, always showed up when I needed her, and never expected me to be anything other than what I was. She remained my friend for a few years. It was actually only after I was grown up that I realized she had been imaginary. One day I asked my mom if she ever found out what happened to this girl as I had never heard where she had gone. My mom seemed quite surprised that I had not realized she was just a manifestation of my imagination. I was somewhat saddened to hear that she was not real because she had been a big part of my life, and had been the one person I really enjoyed spending time with. We mostly just walked and talked, or would take turns pushing each other on the swings. She was beautiful, and always calm and peaceful. The time I spent with this friend are still some of the most vivid memories from that time in my life, and I still think of her on occasion, and miss her. Her friendship helped me get through some very sad and lonely days. I will be forever thankful that she came to be such a trusted friend. I have heard it said that imaginary friends are actually our guardian angels.

But, so began the habit of shutting down, locking in the hurt, while continuing to smile and interact in the present. So began the emergence of the "me" that could show the world one version of me while protecting the other, more fragile version of me. If this sounds like you, please take advantage of the free 15 minute discovery session, one on one, with me.

Go to www.ijustwanttobehappybook.com to sign up for your complimentary session.

"You never know how strong
You are until strong is
Your only choice"
Bob Marley

People can become very good at playing the game of life. The problem with mastering this game is that eventually it becomes your life. It's like that old saying "Be careful what you wish for because you might just get it." You wish for the ache inside you to stop, you wish you could go back to the way things were, you wish you could feel normal again. Slowly but surely life goes on, and you have to figure out your own way to be part of it again. As I mentioned earlier, you continue doing the things that must be done, but with each passing day that list continues to grow as life returns to the daily routine of it all. In the early days we just have to get through the basics of life such as eating, sleeping and daily hygiene. Then we have to get dressed, go back to school, rejoin our activities, go to appointments, those kinds of things. These things are expected of you in such a short time after losing a loved one. Teachers expect you to be at school, your boss expects you to be at work, and stay there all day. Coaches expect you to listen and participate in your sports. Piano teachers expect that you are hearing and learning. All the while you are exhausted, unable to concentrate, and barely have the ability to be there, let alone to live up to the requirements of each task. However, these things are all part of life, and you do find a way. You learn to play the game and master it a little bit more each day.

You learn to answer when spoken to, you learn to smile when someone looks at you, and you learn to interact with others even if those interactions are shallow and meaningless. You learn very quickly what other people want from you and how to oblige. You learn to keep putting one foot in front of the other. What you are really learning through all of this is how to play the game; and the better we can play the easier things will be. People will see that you are fine, and then they will stop asking you every time they see you. You learn you can re-enter the world again, but this time in a very cautious, secluded way. This time you know how much life can hurt, you understand things will change, and that there are things in life that are very unfair.

I no longer had the luxury of being a carefree child, free of worry, pain or guilt. My rose-coloured glasses were gone, and I could now see that dangers were present in everything I did and everywhere I went. So distance is good; it keeps you emotionally protected and buffers the harsh realities of life. The game is helpful because it assists those around you to move on, and it helps you to continue living, even if it no longer seems real. The game can be dangerous...

I remember my 6th birthday very well. Our family was not a wealthy family by any means but my parents always made sure we had everything we needed, and almost everything we wanted. However, birthdays and Christmases were modest, especially by today's terms. We usually received one gift from our parents for our birthday, and at Christmas one gift from our parents and our special gift from Santa. My 6th birthday, however, was extraordinary. I got a new swing set with a slide attached, a "Chrissy" doll with hair that could grow from short to long, and tickets for the entire family to go to the circus. Indeed, this was an extravagant amount of gifts. I knew, as did my siblings, why my parents had gone overboard with the gift giving. It had been one year since my brother's death and they were trying desperately to have me enjoy my birthday. I did my best to be happy, for they had tried so hard to make it a special day for me that I could not bear to let them see how sad I really was. I knew they had to be suffering as well, but we all did our best to be as happy as we could possibly be on that day.

Their love for me still astounds me. On a day that was certainly unbearable for them, they had put my happiness ahead of their sorrow. This is truly the meaning of parents...to love another so much that you deny yourself what you need the most to provide what your child needs. I know how much their hearts were hurting that day, but they hid their sadness in an effort to create a few moments of happiness for me. I think my love for them doubled on that day.

It is in these tiny moments that great lessons are learned. Their strength and their love moved me that day. I believe it was that day that I came to value strength and courage. My mother changed after my brother's death. She became a much more outspoken person. She was often heard saying things like "You were not put in this world to take crap from other people." Her confidence in herself and her abilities grew. In later years we often spoke of the fact that my little brother and I had a very different set of parents than my four older siblings. I was raised to speak confidently, to stick up for those who were unable to do it for themselves, and to be kind but not weak. Honesty was very important in our home as well. I was expected to befriend all the kids at school who had no friends or who got picked on, and to stand up to the bullies. Our family took care of each other as well, and we would defend each other always. We could, and did, fight with each other, but God help the outsider who tried to pick a fight with any one of us.

Being close and relying on each other helped, but it also made it easier for us to hide our hurts and our truths. We all built walls to protect ourselves. We didn't need to rely on other people because we had each other. I'm sure to the outside world it would have seemed that we were doing just fine, and for the most part we were, at least on the surface. Underneath, though, things were still happening. Beliefs were being formed that would last a lifetime, hearts were being hardened, and the hurts and truths were being denied. I know for myself these were not conscious decisions I was making. I don't think any of us decided to change purposefully. It's just what happens when your heart is broken. Your body and mind will find a way to protect you and get you through it. *If you are looking for support from others that have known what you're feeling, please visit my private Facebook group, Healing Your Way to Happiness.*

If you have ever lost anyone close to you then undoubtedly you have heard the adage that "Time heals all wounds." You will also have figured out that this statement is very untrue. Time helps but it most certainly does not heal. The more time passes, the more dull both the heartache and the person suffering the heartache become. You no longer have an open, gaping wound that is visible to the outside world, but you do have a severe scar that limits you deeply. However, as time goes by, you may get to the point where even you can no longer see the scar, and it becomes such a deeply engrained part of you that you often don't even realize that it still remains.

This scar, over time, changes who you are. Think of a physical scar you have on your body. Take note of that scar now. The skin tissue is very different than the skin that has not been damaged. While the scar is tight, unyielding, and seems to be unable to take on the characteristics of your normal skin, so it is with your emotional scars as well. They lay dormant, no longer causing severe pain to you on the outer conscious level of your being, but beneath the surface they are also tight, unyielding and unable to take on the characteristics of the previous you. With time, they effectively deaden the pain you once knew and endeavor to keep you from feeling that pain in the future. When my brother died, I cried; actually my entire body sobbed, but from that day forward, I never cried in sadness again, for many, many years. My grandparents passed away a few years later; I was about 9 years old, and I never shed a single tear. In fact, I remember standing outside the church after my Grandpa's funeral, feeling very removed from the present moment, and just watching my cousins. They were for the most part very distraught. There was a lot of crying, upset and deep emotion being displayed by young and old alike. I remember standing off to the side, alone, and just watching in wonder. Wondering how they could feel such sadness, why they were able to cry for something that just wasn't that sad, and trying to understand why they couldn't see that this death was not a heartbreaking death. I stood in silence, wondering if I was the only person who felt this way, and knew that when an old man died it was not a deeply life-changing sadness. In that moment I did feel alone, and I realized that even though I was young, I now saw things very differently from other people. My Grandpa was 81 years old and it was his time to go, after having lived a long, successful life.

Many more years passed, and several funerals, without me shedding a tear. I lost various people in my life, but was never saddened to the core the way I was when my brother died. Then when my youngest daughter was about 3 years old my cousin's daughter, Laura, passed away from a brain tumour. I, of course, went to her funeral, but totally expected to feel deadened to the pain. I hadn't even bothered to put tissue in my purse as I really never thought I would cry. As I sat in the church with my daughter on my lap, listening to the service, I became completely overwhelmed with a flood of emotion. I began to sob uncontrollably as years' worth of buried emotion flowed from my body. I was shocked by how affected I was. I had forgotten that I was capable of such emotion. I realized at that moment that I was crying for my brother, my parents, my siblings, my grandparents, my cousins, my aunts and uncles, his daughter, his other children, for him and his wife, and the heartbreak his family would have to live through, and all of the people I had lost since age 5.

So while time lessens the pain from day to day, it certainly doesn't heal your wounds. Time allows us to move on, put one foot in front of the other a little stronger each day, and to survive but not to heal. Healing comes from within, and it will only happen when you decide you are ready. Each of you will make your own path, and none of you will have the same path, but you need to get there at your own pace, in your own time, and on your own schedule. There will be many things you have to encounter, learn, and move past before you are ready to let the healing happen.

Visit www.ijustwanttobehappybook.com to learn more about personal coaching, and to see if it seems right for you. Please feel free to register for a Free 15 minute, one on one, discovery session with me, Canada's #1 Empowerment Authority..

This step comes much later, the fake it till you make it technique. Once you've mastered shutting down, playing the game, hiding the hurt, and time has dulled you. This can also become a way of life and can serve you well. You can become a new you using this tool. It works in school, in your relationships, in your career, in any aspect of your life really. The problem with this technique is that at some point you forget you're faking, and the real you stays hidden beneath the fake you. Again, this is very useful if your goal is to protect yourself from being vulnerable, but can be very harmful because no one gets to know the "real" you.

I found I even use this with my family. To them this is known as the "smile and nod" which I mentioned previously. I can interact and look like I'm engaged without ever having to give something of myself. It's easy; it takes very little effort but appeases my siblings very nicely. It can really be used in any conversational topic and reduces stress for me within the conversation. As we've gotten older, and have varied life experiences, we have grown further apart. I often feel there is jealousy between my siblings, and there is a very strong need to be heard, to be right, and to be in control...to be the boss of any given situation. Some of us are more passive-aggressive than others but we still seem to have this need within all of us. This tends to cause a lot of hurt feelings and resentment between siblings. Sometimes we confuse support with dictating the right answer.

Over the years, we have all assumed roles within our family. I know that I keep my distance so that I don't get sucked into the drama. Don't get me wrong; we love each other very much, and I would go to the ends of the earth for each one of them, and them for me, but it is so much easier to not let them in because they will judge, criticize, condemn, and misunderstand, even though they don't mean to. We all have our roles, and we have all created our own patterns and belief systems, and they have become vastly different. The thing that remains the same is that we can be a bossy, judgmental bunch with a strong desire for control. This can make getting together a challenge and so this is the reason I have adopted the "smile and nod."

Even when I started my new business, started writing this book, and taking a bunch of courses, I found it hard to share with my family. I felt that I needed to wait until everything was complete, until I was earning money and being successful. I know that a lot of these issues come from my own beliefs, and I have been working on changing them. Interestingly, my family was quite interested and supportive of my new path. Sometimes what we see in the world is just a mirror of what we see inside of us. So when you see something you don't like, take a minute and ask yourself if that is what you see in that other person, or if perhaps you are projecting your own thoughts and beliefs outwards towards them. *Forgiveness is the key, so if you may be holding onto past hurt, please download this free pdf www.ijustwanttobehappybook.com and click on forgiveness article to start your journey to forgiveness and happiness. I have also included a free downloadable "reframing" PDF for you to use to consciously become aware of your negative self-talk, so you can use it to start changing your language and reframing those thoughts to be more positive. Visitwww.ijustwanttobehappybook.com A Practical Guide To Reframing Your Thoughts For A Happier You.*

Chapter 6

The UN Sadness

Guarding your heart becomes very important once it's been broken. The fewer people you let in, the fewer people that can rip it apart again. I think this happened gradually to me and I didn't really realize that I was doing it. Back to my make-believe friend. I named her Helen and she had beautiful, long, dark hair like I did. I recreated another me that I felt 100% safe with, to share my life with. If that's not guarding your heart – what is? She was the only person I trusted to share my life with. I could tell her anything and there was no judgement. The thing is, from the outside if you had been an observer you would never have known that I wasn't a happy, playful child because outwardly that's how it seemed. I spent lots of time with friends; I was always around people, interacting with them. But it was on a very superficial level. I just joined in because I knew I needed to act and look normal. That was the way you were expected to be. It is very easy to be with people and share nothing about yourself. I think that's the part that astounds me the most. How did I make it through life with no one ever knowing, myself included, that I was hiding? Even now, I have what people would consider to be friends, and yet these friends know very little about my life. They know I have lived here for

25 years, they know I'm married, they know I have four children, they know the ins and outs of daily life that I, and all of us, present to the world. But, as the saying goes, "No one knows what goes on behind closed doors." Each person is a closed door if they choose to be. It is easy to keep the door closed. It's easy to chat about the weather, and work, and all that superficial day-to-day living like the kids and their sports, their school, their boyfriends and girlfriends. A lot of time can be spent talking about superficial stuff. When is the last time that you can think of that you shared something deep and personal about your life with someone? I couldn't tell you the last time I shared something like that. I find it difficult to even share those things with my husband, and we've been married 27 years. Surely he is the one person who knows me the best and yet I have managed to keep him at arm's length too. Guarding your heart is the best way I know to be able to live a superficial life and go on as though nothing is wrong. If you show enough confidence in yourself to the outer world, people do not know what happens behind closed doors.

When you have suffered the kind of pain that I suffered at such an early age, it does become a big secret and you suffer silently. It's too painful to share; it's too scary to talk about. And it's really scary to expose the depths of your pain to other people. They just cannot grasp the intensity of the pain and sorrow that you are feeling. That becomes very frustrating; you can't grasp their ability to continue on as though nothing happened, and they can't grasp your ability to need to stay behind, to need to stay where you feel that pain. I guess the feeling of pain is really the only thing you have to make you feel real, to make you feel alive. It's almost like you hold onto the pain to hold onto the person that you've lost. It's like you're afraid that if you move on, you're leaving that person behind. I come back to my make-believe friend, Helen. We spent many hours together playing, swinging, laying in the grass, just being...with no expectation. She was the one person I could totally be myself around, and that I could share all of my secrets with. I could tell her anything, and not have to worry. She just understood me completely; she was the only person in my life who did understand me completely. You know, there is a saying that people come into your life for a reason or a season; she definitely came into my life for both a reason and a season. She was my best friend for a long time. Maybe through me sharing this story, it will help you understand the depth of pain that I was feeling at that time, how much I felt that I could not share that pain with the outside world because people just didn't get it. They didn't get me, they didn't understand, they had no way of understanding. My friends were kids too, they were 5 as well, and they hadn't experienced what I had, so they had no way to really understand what I had gone through or how I was feeling. So I manifested a friend that completely understood me inside and out. It is shocking to me that my parents and my siblings never knew about this friend for a long time, but none of my siblings was close to my age, and all of them were doing different stuff than I was. So, I relied on this friend very much to share this secret pain because she was the only person in my world that got exactly where I was coming from and understood exactly how I felt. I could totally be myself with her and say anything, and yet I don't remember being sad with her. I remember being peaceful. When she left my life, I was more able to deal with the outside world, but I had learned by that point not to share my pain and my feelings. To just go on and act normal, and do the things that normal kids my age would do. I don't blame people; none of this is about blame. This is about realizing many, many years later how I got to be where I was. And again, it is not that where I ended up was a bad place. I have a great marriage, I have 4 wonderful children, we have a beautiful home, but I wasn't happy. I looked happy and I had happy moments but I was not a happy person. I think that over time I told myself that I couldn't be happy, that I believed so strongly in the pain I had carried around silently that I just didn't believe I would ever know true happiness. I think there are a lot of people like me out in the world, just going through the motions. We live our daily lives and we just don't know what we don't know. We think the lives that we are living are the normal lives of all the people in the world, and we are no different than anybody else. I actually agree with that to some extent; I think we are having an epidemic in that human beings have forgotten how to be happy. We are so worried about our careers, our homes, how we look to the community, our successes. We think that these things will bring us happiness so we always end up chasing happiness instead of enjoying life in every moment. *Be sure to download your free copy of my "Happiness Handbook" if you have not done so yet at www.ijustwanttobehappybook.com.*

My heart certainly did harden over the years. Even my own father, who I consider to be my soul mate, has sometimes said to me that I am cold-hearted and hard-hearted. The rules are the rules; I expected people to follow the rules, I expected my children to do as they were asked. I was a strict parent, but a very loving parent. But I didn't believe in having to ask twice. Many years ago I worked as a resource teacher for special needs children, and I attended a seminar in which the speaker asked "How many of you ever ask your children to do something more than once?" Of course we all put our hands up. His point in this exercise was that as parents we only expect our children to do as they are asked 50% of the time. This stayed with me. It is not that my children were perfect, and it's not that they did what they were asked the first time every time, but I have to admit they were very, very well-trained. When they were asked to do something, they knew the expectation was that it would get done. Now, my son always challenged that. He was a bit of a free spirit compared to my girls. He definitely had a mind of his own, and his mind definitely worked in a different way than mine. He would rather take a consequence for not doing as he was asked if he was enjoying doing what he was doing. Through my son I learned a lot of lessons. What I have discovered in the past 5 years is that children are wonderful teachers to their parents. I've learned a lot of life lessons from my children. Sadly, my children have also learned a lot of life lessons from me, and one of those is burying your emotions. So becoming stone, to me, means that nothing gets in and nothing gets out. You have barricaded your heart behind a stone covering. I became cold in many ways, and I was sometimes unapproachable, but again, I think that was a survival tactic. It happened over time and it just was a protective covering; almost a very stoic personality. By definition stoic simply means a person who can endure pain and hardship without showing their feelings or complaining, or being free from passion, being unmoved by either joy or grief. That really sums up the person I became. There are quotes saying those who know the deepest sorrow, are the ones who will also have pure joy. I don't think this is always true; for me that was not the case. I had become indifferent to pleasure or pain; physical pain as well as emotional pain. I didn't believe there is a need for me to be sick, I didn't believe there was a need for me to baby myself. If I have a sore back, I just keep moving, knowing it'll free up. I don't believe in spending a day in bed because I have a cold or the flu. When I was pregnant I was always saying "I'm not sick, I'm pregnant. I'm fine; I can do everything I have always done." I have never pampered myself. There are many women who go for massages, pedicures, manicures, facials, spa treatments etc. These were not things that I did, and not because I was denying myself, but simply because it never occurred to me that I needed to do those things. When I began my sessions with my life coach, one of the first homework assignments he gave me was to go get a massage because he felt it would help me get in touch with my emotions. I remember distinctly telling him that I don't like emotions. I didn't want to get in touch with my emotions; they were fine just where they were. I never thought of myself as a stoic person, but by nature of definition, it definitely is the person I became. That is a very sad state to be in; to be a person who is unmoved by joy or grief. Life is meant to have joy, life is meant to be fun! But again, it wasn't that I was denying myself those things; it was that at some very deep level, I didn't believe in those things, I didn't believe that life was meant to be fun. I didn't believe that life was meant to be filled with joy. I believed that life was hard work. That it was meant to be hard work, and therefore, by being a very hard worker, that was my way of being successful in life. I could pat myself on the back at the end of the day and say "Boy, I worked hard; I started work before everybody and I finished long after everybody," and hard work was my reward. Each time a behavior is reinforced it becomes more deeply engrained. I remember one day we were moving our head office location, and I was moving all kinds of boxes and lifting things that were very heavy, and I ended up putting my back out because I have some sciatic nerve damage. The next day I showed up to work and was moving tenderly and slowly. Two co-workers saw me coming into the office building and said, "Oh Helen, you should go home, you shouldn't be at work," and I responded by saying "Why would I go home? A sore back is going to hurt just as much at home as it is at work, so no sense staying home, I've got work to do." Those things, I have since learned, are not normal behavior for most people. However, I chose to ignore the pain, I chose to ignore my own body's warning signs that I needed to change. Luckily I was able to persevere through it, and my belief in not pampering myself worked for me. I only had a sore back for a couple of days, and was back to normal and able to continue on, and never missed a beat.

Our own bodies give us warning signs. During that same time

period, I had a large bald spot appear out of nowhere on the back of my head, probably about the size of a lacrosse ball. I woke up one morning, went to the hairdresser to get my monthly haircut, and as she was cutting she yelled out "Oh shit!" Of course, that rather startled me so I asked what happened, thinking she had cut too much or something, and she held up a mirror and showed me this nice, shiny bald spot on the back of my head. Again, my body was trying to tell me that I was overdoing it, but I chose to ignore that and continued to overdo it. I did go to see my homeopath, and luckily my hair did grow back in, but it was extremely fine, like a new baby's hair, and pure white. So for almost a year, I had a very thin patch of pure white hair on the back of my head, surrounded by dark brown hair everywhere else. It did all come back normally over time, but the point is that I refused to see that my body was telling me I needed a break; I refused to see that I was stressed, and I refused to see that perhaps I needed help, and chose to believe that I could do it and that I was fine. I believed I knew the answers, and I just had to continue on and everything would be fine.

I judged other people's sorrow on a scale, always compared to the sorrow I had been through, as well as how they reacted to sorrow. I honestly didn't think of this as a selfish act, or an unkind thing to do. I could empathize with them for the pain they were feeling, but then I would judge them for it. I worked with a lady who lost her mother, and each year on the anniversary of her mother's death she took the day off work. I judged this, and thought of her as weak. I never once thought that perhaps she was allowing herself to take the day to truly celebrate her mother and her mother's life for everything it meant to her. I understand now that it was not up to me to judge how another person deals with their personal hurt and loss. Logically I understood this, but internally I judged her and her actions.

I also judged the smaller things in life. One time my sister-in-law was baking a cake for some sort of special event. When she took the cake out of the oven it slipped and she dropped it. She cried when she saw the sight of her freshly baked cake upside down on the floor. This behavior truly did shock me – I was annoyed though that someone would actually cry because they dropped a cake. Life will definitely go on without as much as a hiccup without a cake to serve your guests. In this type of incident I must say that I could not empathize; I could sympathize but not empathize. I just could not get my head around being emotional about something that I viewed as so trivial. The thing is – I viewed it as trivial, she did not, and it is not up to another person to tell you what to feel, how to react, or when to be emotional. This was definitely my issue, not hers, but at that time I could not even see it from her perspective. I had no understanding at all of how she felt in that moment.

This type of incident happens every day in life, sometimes at work, sometimes in a social setting or with family. I went through most of my married life, at least a good 25 years, judging other people on the hurt or loss they felt, as well as how they reacted to it. This was not

an intentional action on my part; it was an underlying limiting belief that I didn't even recognize for many years. I never thought that I was dismissing their feelings; I just honestly could not understand their grief or loss because from my perspective it seemed quite insignificant.

I also judged my own emotions to daily life by the same standard. I think that somehow as long as I judged everyone by the same set of rules, I felt justified in my perspective. It was not that I allowed myself to indulge in emotions, and then judged others for the same behavior; it is that I judged every person, including myself, for having a lapse in their emotional state. I guess the strangest part of this for me now is that not once did I see that perhaps they were reacting the way people should react, and I was the one that was abnormal. Now that I have begun to heal I can see clearly that it was me that was being irrational. My behavior was abnormal; I was the one that needed to learn to be softer, kinder and more supportive of myself as well as those around me. I can also see that I was sabotaging my own happiness by holding onto my hurt so tightly that I could not even feel another person's pain.

Mental health was a very difficult issue for me to understand. I could not logically grasp the fact that someone could be so emotionally vulnerable. I could not identify with someone that could feel so raw. I could be sympathetic, and know that something in their life must be terribly wrong, but I could not identify with the emotion they were feeling. Intellectually I knew that they were suffering, but

I had no recognition of how. I put it down to the fact that some people are just made of sturdier stock; as my aunt said to my sister when her son died "You come from a long line of tough old birds." This is how I made sense of mental health. My youngest daughter and my son had a friend that battled with depression; he lost his battle during his 1st year of University. She was completely overwhelmed and distraught when she heard of his death. She, my son, and I had many discussions surrounding his death, and trying to make sense of it in some way. I tried to explain this to my youngest daughter, who is my emotional child, as a way for her to make sense of things when her friend lost his battle.. Again, our children are wonderful teachers, and she refused to accept this as an explanation. Through her and the experience of her losing her friend Steven Hutchison, to mental illness, I have gained a much healthier awareness for mental illness. However, it was not until I went through my own coaching that I understood I was as emotionally broken as anyone else with a mental illness. While they had so much raw emotion, pain and suffering, I was unable to feel emotion, pain or suffering. It was two extreme ends of the same emotional scale, and neither end creates healthy, happy people.

I have since lived through recurring suicidal attempts with someone very near and dear to my heart, and every day I am truly grateful that I was no longer working, had been through personal coaching and had begun to heal myself, and had become a certified coach so that I could help him throughout his own private battle. I believe very strongly that the Universe gives us what we need and provides us with opportunity if we have the wherewithal to see it. I am also extremely grateful to all those who have battled mental illness, their families, their communities and the special people who make mental health awareness a priority. The sadness in our world is growing day by day, and awareness is key. I also firmly believe that our educational system needs to find a way to have a much happier, kinder environment for our children, and that if mental health awareness and life coaching were available as part of the curriculum in primary school, our teenagers would be much better equipped to deal with the pressures of today's world, therefore making our young adults more balanced, stress free, happy, motivated, loving individuals mentally prepared to raise the next generation. I have included a guided meditation for you by Lisa Nicholls, star of the hit movie "The Secret." *I encourage you to listen and enjoy her wonderful healing, simply go to www.ijustwanttobehappybook.com to listen to the guided-meditation.*

Chapter 7

Moments Of Joy

Life does have moments and times of great joy. Falling in love was one of those times for me. I didn't date much in high school, and boys weren't a big priority at that time in my life. I had the occasional date here and there, and I did date one guy for about 6 months. I was only sixteen at the time, and he was much older than I was. He was actually a friend of my brother-in-law's and we met at their college graduation. I believe that I mentioned earlier that I was always more comfortable with adults than people my own age, so it is really not surprising that I dated someone older. What was surprising is that my parents allowed it.

After this relationship I stayed single, and pretty much out of the dating seen for about four years. I had quit high school and started working when I was sixteen so for the next couple of years I wasn't really around people my own age that much. I started college at 18 and lived with 5 other people in a house while going to school. I still went home on weekends to see friends and family so was more social again. There were a lot of dances in the community centre and my friends were beginning to get married.

I knew my husband then, and had for several years because he and my sister were friends. He and I ended up at a lot of the same events and had mutual friends. I thought he was kind of a show off and didn't really like him. He, on the other hand, was persistent... asking me to dances, sitting and talking to me at parties. One night after a dance where he had too much to drink he was out in front of the arena not doing very well. I was with my girlfriend and my brother. I was the designated driver in my little Chevette. I decided we couldn't leave him there by himself so my brother and I loaded him up into my car, but before we could get him in he threw up all over my shoes. Getting him in the car was not an easy task, as he was 6'2" and about 220 lbs. We finally got him in and took him to his friend's where he was staying for the night. My girlfriend was going into the house to see if she could find some help to get him out of the car but my brother assured her that I would be just fine, so the two of them continued on to join the party. I managed to get him out of the car and into the house. We spent the remainder of the night just talking with each other. It turned out that his girlfriend at the time was to have come with him for the weekend, and for whatever reason did not.

Sometime later he called me and asked me on a date. I declined but he called again the next weekend. My mother felt it was necessary to offer me some advice. She said I should "just go out with him if he called again, as he would find out what a bitch I could be and then it would be over." Now this may sound harsh, but remember, we are a close family that values honesty, and I really think she thought that would be the easiest way to get him to stop calling. Plus, she really liked him, and I think she was secretly hoping that it would work out. So he called again to invite me to a friend's wedding. I agreed. We dated for four months, and then he went on a cruise with some friends. While he was away I was trying to decide what to do with my life. When he returned from his cruise I realized I had missed him, which rather surprised me. February 29th, 1988, I asked him to marry me. It was Sadie Hawkins day, so I decided that day that I would pop the question. I planned a romantic evening with dinner out, but when I called to invite him he wasn't home. I continued to call him periodically throughout the evening but no answer. Finally I gave up and drove home to my parents' house. My dad was the only one home that night, so I ended up spending the evening with him. This time it was Dad's turn to give the advice. His advice was "If this is really what you want don't give up." So together my dad and I said a little prayer and I called my boyfriend one more time. This time he answered. We chatted for a bit on the phone and then I asked if he would marry me. I told him the offer was only valid until midnight, and it was after 11:00 p.m. when he finally answered the phone. I think he was a bit shocked by it all, but said yes. Six months later, August 6, 1988, we were married. This truly was one of the happiest days of my life.

We had planned on having an outdoor wedding, but our church had a change in priests. The new priest was not a missionary so could not perform a ceremony outside of the church. I had already purchased my wedding dress. We had a large wedding party, 17 people in all. The girls wore red taffeta cocktail length dresses. The guys had white tuxedos and Ken wore a tailcoat. My two nieces were flower girls and my oldest nephew and Godson was the ring bearer.

Ken had both his brothers, my brother and his closest friends stand up with him. I had my three sisters, two childhood friends, and a college roommate. Our families went to an incredible amount of work for our wedding. My dad spent countless hours working on the yard, watering the grass, trimming the hedges and getting everything picture perfect. My parents made all of the food for the dinner, and we had 525 guests so that was no small endeavor. Ken's mom made an incredible wedding cake, and all the flowers for the wedding. My sisters helped decorate, and graciously donated their time, money and decorations for the wedding. Everything turned out beautifully!

When we were married it was customary for the bride and groom to leave the reception, change into their going away outfits, and then head off for the honeymoon. Neither my husband nor I wanted to leave our own party, so we went and changed, then returned to enjoy the remainder of the reception. We ended up spending the night at my parents', slept in a tent trailer and spent the entire next day with family and friends. We had a huge brunch with many of our wedding guests. Later on that day we packed up our gifts and headed to our apartment in Brampton to start our life together.

We did go away for a short honeymoon. We spent two nights at a beautiful resort close to home. We enjoyed the time there, but we really wanted to get back home. I had the wedding of my dreams, with the man of my dreams; life could not have been any better. It is funny how things work out sometimes.

We had discussed children before we got married and decided we would wait five years before beginning our family. We were both young and felt it would be good to wait until we could move out of the city and buy a house before having kids. Also we felt that it would be good to have some time as a couple before becoming parents. Well, just over a year later on August 20, 1989, we were blessed with our first child. We had talked about names, and I felt very strongly that the names we chose would be names of strong, independent people. Our first child was a beautiful baby girl; we named her Joni (pronounced Johnny) Frances Batte. She was named after my dad and Ken's mom. It is truly incredible how much love you have for a child; my heart expanded that day and I don't think that I fully understood before her birth how much you could love another human being.

Thirteen months later we had our second child, also a daughter. Another beautiful little girl, Jami Elizabeth Batte, was granted to us on October 2, 1990. She was perhaps the most glowing baby I had ever seen. She was absolutely peaceful from the moment she was born. She had dark hair, and a rosy pink skin. She was born quickly; my labour started at midnight and by 2:00 a.m. she had entered the world. Her sister had taken much longer, a 32 hour labour. Joni was content to stay safe and warm in the womb.

Life was good; we had two beautiful daughters and our family was doing well. I had returned to work after each child and had also returned to school. I worked full-time and went to school 2 – 3 times per week from the time Joni, the oldest, was 6 months old. Ken was still working in Brampton and commuting daily from Arthur. His days were long and with two babies, our nights were short.

On July 6, 1992 we had our third child; this time a gorgeous baby boy. There were 21 months between Jami and Joe. Joseph Alphonse Batte joined our family and his sisters were pleased with their new baby. Joe didn't sleep much; we were lucky if he slept from midnight to 4:00 a.m. He was a snuggly baby and loved to be held. He was 7 lbs 1 oz at birth but grew quickly, and was 20 lbs by five months of age. This little bundle of joy was the perfect addition to our growing family. With each child my heart expanded and I realized just how much love is within.

Finally our fourth child came on February 3, 1994, 17 months after her brother. As mentioned previously, this pregnancy was challenging. I was extremely healthy and very active, and had only gained 14 lbs during the pregnancy. We didn't have a name picked yet when she was born; we just couldn't find a name that we both loved. It was tradition that after the birth of each of our children, Ken would go and pick up the other kids and bring them to the hospital so that we could bring the newest addition to our family home together. When he returned to the hospital with Joni, Jami and Joe, they each had a turn to hold their new baby sister. The girls suggested we name her Jerica, from a TV show they had watched with their cousin. Ken and I both liked the name, and so our youngest child was named Jerica Helen Batte, born weighing 7 lbs 3 oz, and the picture of health.

Our family was now complete. Ken didn't think he could handle another pregnancy if it was as stressful as the last one. We agreed that four children were enough, and we had been blessed each time with healthy, beautiful babies. Our children have been the most incredible part of my life, and the most precious.

I cannot imagine my life without their love. Every time I look at them I am grateful for everything they have brought into my life. They have grown into beautiful, caring adults and through them I have learned some of life's greatest lessons. I am thankful that my husband and I together have had the opportunity to have raised four such wonderful people, who we now consider to be our closest friends.

Being a parent is easily the most rewarding act in my life. It is also the hardest, most demanding, tiring, never-ending job I have ever had. I cannot imagine the past twenty six years of my life if I had not been fortunate enough to be a mother. I love being a mother more than anything else in life. Motherhood without a doubt was my truest purpose.

Kids are the most affectionate, open, honest, wonderful individuals on earth. They are also some of the very best teachers you will ever meet. They teach you how to love unconditionally, how to share, how to treat one another, and so many other countless lessons. I am still learning life lessons constantly from my children. It is incredible how four people can change you, challenge you, make you grow, and improve your life so much. The love you have for a child is unparalleled from any other love in the world.

My kids are my world, even to this day. I am extremely close to all of my children, and truly miss them if we have to go even a few days without talking or seeing each other. Thankfully we all live close to one another. Two still live at home, one lives in the same town, and one splits her time currently between school in Hamilton and home. When they started leaving home to go to university it was hard; good but hard. My two oldest left the same weekend to start school; one moved to Waterloo and the other to Ottawa. Ottawa seemed so far away, and she was young, only 17 years old. She came home as often as possible, though, which helped.

Now our family is growing again. Our youngest daughter Jerica is engaged. Jami married this summer on July 16, 2016 and Jerica will be married in the summer of 2017, on July 29th. We are extremely fortunate to have two such wonderful young men joining our inner circle; Alex Kramp and Luke Raftis. There is no limit to the size of one's heart, or the size of one's family. I am excited to be entering a new phase of life and cannot wait to become a grandma. There is never a happier time in my life than when our home is filled with the energy and joy of small children.

Chapter 8

Giving Up

Perhaps unhappiness is not the correct term, as I was not unhappy in life, in my marriage, in my career. I was content and things were going along as expected. I think maybe a more accurate term would be that I felt "an absence of happiness." I love my husband and we have a good relationship, but yet it felt like it could have been better. I love my kids and very much enjoy spending time with them, but it still seemed as though things could have been better. I liked my career and the people I worked with, but something was missing. I am a person who has deep faith, but my spirituality was not what it should have been. Financially things were better than ever before but still not where I wanted to be, and it brought little joy. Everything in my life was good but it just felt dull. There was no vibrancy, no joy, and no excitement. Even when we were out having fun with other couples I couldn't help but feel as though somehow it should feel different. Why was I not enjoying myself? What was missing?

It sounds crazy; most people would enjoy my life, so why didn't I? It was funny though; my husband felt the same way and I never knew it. While my husband and I were being interviewed by the coaching company I had contacted to see if I was a fit for their coaching program as a potential client, they talked to us both and we discovered at that moment that he was feeling the same way. We had not discussed anything ahead of time as we had no idea what kind of questions would be asked in the interview. We both just felt that basically there should be something better. We both wanted better relationships with our siblings, we both wanted to have more fun, and we both felt that even though things were good everything felt very lackluster.

We decided at that point that I would sign up and start with a Life Coach, and it was the best decision we could have made. Since my coaching I have written this book, learned some incredible stock market trading techniques, learned about several investment opportunities, become a certified stage speaker, created a website, learned about real estate, wealth creation and management and become a Certified Coach. None of this even compares to what I learned in my own personal coaching. I have been able to change my own mindset and now can see the world and everything in it from a very different perspective. I have been able to let go of all the resentment and guilt that I had been hanging onto for a lifetime. I have learned to forgive myself, and therefore have no need to forgive anyone else as that need dissipated from within me as soon as I was able to forgive me.

My life has changed tremendously in a very short time, and I am now excited about the person I am becoming. Change is simple, but not easy. It can be scary but it is worthwhile. I am so much happier. The biggest changes I have made in my life are the smallest things. It is simply being aware of your own thoughts each moment; it is having the courage to change those thoughts, and the most powerful change of all is learning to be present in each moment. I can now truly enjoy my life because I am no longer living in the past or worrying about the future which means I can take each day, and each moment within the day and appreciate it fully. *To learn how to appreciate the present moment, download my free "Happiness Handbook" at www.ijustwanttobehappybook.com and take advantage of the tips and tools you will learn to use in your everyday life to increase your happiness now.*

Do you ever feel there should be more to life? Maybe it's because our children are grown, or maybe it's because I am getting older and thought that life would have been more fun, or maybe it's because I don't want to wait another twenty years until retirement to start having fun, but I feel that there should be more to life than mundane daily living.

My sister asked me recently if I was having a midlife crisis. I laughed at her notion, but who knows; I guess you could call it that. Maybe that's what a midlife crisis is and why people go through them. I'm not looking for a younger man, or a sexy sports car, but I am looking for something. I am looking for a change. I want to be more vibrant, more energetic, and happier. I want to be free mentally, emotionally, physically, spiritually and financially.

For interest sake, I did look up the meaning of a midlife crisis. It is a term that was first coined by Elliott Jacques, referring to a critical phase in a personal life during the forties to sixties, based on periods of transition. So by definition I guess that wanting a change in your life at my age could constitute a midlife crisis. I don't think that the term without definition fits the normal pattern of what we generally think of as a midlife crisis.

I see my experience as a quest for change, reflection, and self-improvement. As I said earlier I am a survivor, but I'm tired of just surviving. I am tired of going through the motions and playing the game. I am sick of being caught up in the rat race that life has become for so many. I want to choose my own destiny, create the lifestyle I want, and truly enjoy the rest of my life. I want my husband to be able to retire early if he should so choose; I want to have time and energy to enjoy our grandchildren to the fullest. I want to be able to live life the way we want to live it now not in 20 years from now. I am tired of living but not being alive! *You may have difficulty knowing where to start, so I have included a free "How To Create A Vision Board" download, to assist you in setting your goals, and attaining them. You will learn how to create and use a vision board to assist you in reaching your goals. You can find it at www.ijustwanttobehappy book.com.*

Sometimes it seems as though all you do is work. You spend the majority of your lifetime working for other people, helping them build their business and net worth. Don't get me wrong; there is nothing wrong with that, but it means that you are trading hours of your life for their dollars. For most of my life I just accepted that this is what life is and it was the norm; most people live this way. It was actually the owner from a previous company that I worked for that showed me that this is a crazy way to live. He stayed home and rarely came to the office or worked in the company; if he spent time working it was to work on the company, never in it. All of the employees traded hours for dollars and he accumulated the wealth. None of the employees ever questioned this. He had worked hard to start his company; he had invested the money and took on all of the risk, built it into a successful business, and in doing so he had gained the respect of his employees.

However, when his son joined the business and started to work in the company as an employee, neither the owner nor his son liked the fact that the son was now trading hours for dollars. When he was first hired, I was told that he was to be treated the same as any other employee as he needed to learn the company. This didn't last very long, and the son became bored and unsatisfied. When he showed up late for work, he didn't feel he should be disciplined, he thought it was okay for him to leave early or take long lunches as he was sales, and sales didn't need to be accountable for their time and performance was what counted; however, all the other sales people in the company were expected to be to work on time, and work their full shift. Eventually he was allowed to come and go from the office as he pleased. It was definitely the owner's right to make this decision. Unfortunately, the lesson I was hoping to teach the son is that he should have been earning the respect of his fellow employees so that if and when he took over the company he would be someone they looked up to and trusted. This fell on deaf ears. I learned many valuable lessons from the owner of this company, but this may have been the most valuable one.

I have recently come to understand that most people live by the 80/20 rule, meaning that 20% of your rewards come from 80% of your output (work). People with abundance, however, operate differently, and 80% of their rewards come from 20% of their output (work). Rewards can be financial, time, happiness; anything you find rewarding that you desire more of. Imagine if you could change your life so that 80% of your income was driven by 20% of your output. That would be life-changing for anyone who is not already financially free.

So this is the life I desire, the change I am looking for in all areas of my life. I am learning how to be more efficient in my thinking, much more aggressive in my mindset, and much less busy in ways that do not produce actual results in my life. In short, I am learning to work smarter not harder, and to open myself up to a new way of seeing the world and all of the opportunity it has to offer. The entrepreneurial mindset is very different than the employee mindset. *If you have* trouble grasping this idea, I recommend you read "Rich Dad, Poor Dad" and "The Cashflow Quadrant" by Robert T. Kiyosaki.

I have decided that I am done with letting life pass me by. I am creating my own life, my own choices, and my own destiny. I will decide who I will be, and how my life will unfold. I believe strongly in the law of attraction; the belief that like attracts like. I have set my intentions on a more fulfilling life, and I am working towards that goal each and every day with my goal clearly within sight. *See my new "How to Create A Vision Board" to start setting clear intentions for the life of your dreams. Go to www.ijustwanttobehappybook.com to claim your free up to date copy.*

Chapter 9

Life Is Not Fair

The reality of life is that it's not fair, or so it certainly seemed to me for many years. I bought into this belief at a fairly young age. "Life is not fair; deal with it and move on." "This is the hand you have been dealt in life, make the most of it." I'm sure you too have heard these phrases. In my home and community of people these words were certainly common practice. Along with others such as "Some people are just lucky" or "Don't complain, life can always get worse." As I went about living life I never really thought about what these words meant or how they can affect your life. I have even said these same words to my children.

More recently though, I have been looking at my own life, trying to figure out why I am where I am and how I got here. I never thought of myself as being a victim. I thought I believed in creating my own destiny. However, when I started to listen to the words I used, and the thoughts I carried in my head, I realized this was not accurate. No matter what our conscious thoughts say, until you go deeper and examine your subconscious you will not find the ugly truth that lies beneath the surface, sabotaging your life, your work, your finances, spirituality, and happiness.

With the guidance of a wonderful coach, I have been able to discover all the hidden beliefs I held deeply inside, evaluate them, and peel back the layers that I have accumulated over my lifetime. I have been astonished at how quickly I have been able to change, and how much I've accomplished in such a short time.

When I made the decision to get a life coach, I thought the area I needed the most help with was my financial mindset. I scored myself quite high in the areas of personal development, spirituality, relationships, career, emotional wellbeing and confidence. I thought that if I could just get my financial life to be healthier I'd be set, and life would be great! What I quickly discovered was that my financial life was healthier than most other areas, and until I dealt with the other "stuff" my financial situation was not likely to change.

I discovered that my emotional wellbeing was not healthy. I had created so many blocks that I was an emotional mess underneath, even though no one, not even me, could see it. I had buried so many emotions for so many years; the only emotion I was accustomed to was anger. I had come to depend on anger; it was controllable, it kept me in control, it worked to get me out of almost any type of situation, and it had worked quite well for many years.

What I have noticed now though, after really getting comfortable with my other emotions, is that I am rarely ever angry anymore. Previously in life if things were not working out as I had envisioned I would get a heavy sensation in my chest, followed by outbursts of anger. Now I realize that sensation was stress, and when those feelings arrived I instinctively went into fight, flight or freeze mode. My natural instinct was to fight, and I was pretty good at it too. I could change the vote in a debate, could change almost anyone's mind and have them see it my way, because I refused to give in. People responded to the authoritative voice and stance that came with my anger. There was power with anger and I liked feeling the power.

So, life is not fair because life is what we choose to make it. If you are unsatisfied with your life or a certain aspect of your life you are the only person with the power to change it. Once you understand this and make a conscious choice to do something about it you can have the life of your dreams; any life that you want. Thoughts create feelings, feelings create desire, desire creates the motivation to take action, and action will be the tool used to take you where you want to go in all facets of your life. We cannot simply change our thought process and expect the prize to fall from the sky, but if we change our thoughts, and believe wholeheartedly in our desires, and then take the required action – we can manifest the life of our dreams! *Go to www.ijustwanttobehappybook.com to watch the video - how-to-be-happy-for-ever-and-ever-with-wayne-dyer and learn from one of the greatest personal development mentors of all times.*

Depending on what is going on in your life at any given time you may act differently. In times of stress you tend to be crankier. If you are having a difficult time in your marriage, with your kids, or with work, you will act differently than when things in life are going smoothly. Overall, though, there are periods of time or stages that are characterized by typical behavior. For example, when my children were all in public school I was very different than when they were in high school. As you know I am not a fan of the school system. I was bound and determined to make sure that my children were safe, and treated with respect within that system. As you also know, I had four children within four and a half years. I volunteered weekly in each of the kids' classrooms, went on school trips, was involved in the PTA, helped with special events, and my girlfriend and I were also the "lice ladies" for the entire school. We did monthly head checks in the classrooms, and were on call for breakouts or special cases. So, I spent the majority of my time at the school. There were many reasons I chose to do this. First, I am a resource teacher for special needs children by trade; so I knew I could be of service to the school and the teachers. Second, I love kids and teaching, and third, it was the best way I knew of to have my finger on the pulse of everything that went on inside the school. After having lost so many children I was not willing to have even one child be mistreated, at least not as long as I was present.

The treatment of children is one of my biggest priorities in life. I believe strongly that every child deserves to be treated with dignity and respect. I also believe that respect is earned, not demanded, and that teachers as the professionals and the adults, are the leaders and need to earn the respect of the children they are educating. To me leadership is very different than managing or being in authority. There were a few amazing teachers in our school (and that is because they were amazing people), but we had a much larger number that were average or less than average in my opinion.

I was willing to put in as many hours as needed to help the kids, the teachers and the school, but I was absolutely unwilling to see children be mistreated. Over the years I had many disagreements and downright battles with various vice principals, principals and the school board. There were abusive teachers in this school as well, and again I was dismayed at how many times teachers would simply close their doors, their eyes, and their ears to the abuse that was happening. Children were being degraded, belittled, ridiculed and bullied by teachers on a regular basis. The children who had the nerve to say something back were put in the hall or sent to spend the day at the principal's office.

The person I became in those years was not always kind, patient or forgiving. More than once I raised hell and put a prop under it, and it would remedy the situation presently at hand, but didn't do much in the end to actually change the system or those that worked within it. The union is a powerful entity and unfortunately often protects the wrong people. My advice to all parents is to spend enough time in your child's school to understand first-hand the culture your child is living in on a daily basis. If it is not a healthy environment it is your responsibility to work diligently for change. These are your kids and you must be their champion. It takes a number of years to get four kids through nine grades. I did return to work part-time when my youngest was in grade 3. The following year I started a new position full-time.

Choose wisely as to the type of person you become; your children are watching you and forming their own belief systems about life. Show them you love them; that they can choose happiness and peace over anger and stress. Spend time in their environments and support them by making change where it is needed. Talk to your children and really get to know them. Make sure they understand that you will never give up on them and that they have the power to become whoever and whatever they desire.

My life had, in many ways, become the aftermath of various incidents that led me to where I was just two short years ago. Aftermath - signs or results of an event or occurrence considered collectively, especially of a catastrophe or disaster. This seems to be an adequate description of how I lived my life . I was very thin, was losing my hair, had a rash that covered my entire lower body, and I was physically and mentally exhausted, but too dumb (actually emotionally inept) to recognize it or pay attention to my own body. My husband, my kids and my staff had all been trying to tell me but I didn't listen to them either. I was fine; just a bit tired but otherwise fine. I worked incredibly long hours as I had started a new position about a year previously as Manager of Service Operations and was responsible for the entire company, 11 offices and 50 staff members along with the Manager of Sales Operations. I was head of Service so therefore responsible for everything other than Sales. I really enjoyed this position, and was sure that things would settle down and be manageable sooner than later. I loved working with the staff, encouraging their personal and professional growth, helping them find their strengths, assisting them to become more fulfilled in their positions and their careers. I wanted to spend as much time as I could out in the offices with them, but it was difficult because work just kept piling up. So I could continue getting out to the offices it meant that most nights I worked at home until 11:00 p.m. to keep up with the demands. I never begrudged the work I did at home as I was learning so much and dealing with all kinds of things I had not previously had the opportunity to learn.

I did enjoy both the company that I was employed with, and the position I held. I figured I would retire with this company, and worked as hard as I would have, had it been my own business. I was well-compensated financially as well. However, while I did appreciate my pay cheque and expense allowance I was not motivated by the money. There was a bonus plan but I never counted on the bonus; to me it was just that, a bonus. It didn't motivate me to go above or beyond; it was the staff members that motivated me. They were the reason I loved the job, they were the reason for working the long hours, to change, and to grow. They were an incredible group of women and each one of them added value to my life. I was downsized from this company on April 28, 2015, after almost 13 years of service. This is when I realized my life was an aftermath of various events, and that I needed to change that immediately. I looked back over my life and career, and the following is the path that eventually led me to where I am today.

My career started as resource teacher for special needs children aged 2 through 6. I worked with children in their homes, nursery schools, and daycares, teaching the children and their parent's new skills to help with their development. I love working with children and very much enjoyed my work. After having our third child though, I decided to stay home and raise our children. I was extremely fortunate to be home with our kids for 10 years. I ran a nursery school in our home 2 – 3 days a week from 9:30 – noon for several years. This way I was able to be home with our kids, still do work that I loved, and contribute financially to our household. Nursery school was very structured, and it was set up in our basement away from our children's normal living space and their bedrooms. I had my own toys, tables, play structures, equipment and craft supplies; it was important for me to keep the kids home life separate from the nursery school. When my youngest was entering Grade 3 I decided it was time to take a break. I ended my Nursery School program and took some time off. During this period of time, around the year 2000, I suffered from a very severe head injury. I was painting a big bow window in our home and as I finished for the day and was climbing down the ladder, the ladder tipped over and I fell. I broke all of my ribs on the cement casing of the flower bed and hit my head on the cement sidewalk below, from about 10 feet up. I lost my short-term memory completely. My long-term memory was not affected, thankfully. This was a very difficult thing to deal with. Our kids were all active in various school activities, sports, dance, karate etc. My husband was self-employed at the time and would often need my assistance to do various errands and bookkeeping tasks for him. On more than one occasion I did not show up to pick the kids up for their activities simply because I could not remember where they were or what time they needed to be picked up. To alleviate some of the struggle, Ken and the kids would write sticky notes with all of the things they needed me to do or to attend, and then stick them to my cigarette pack – the one thing I always was sure to have with me. Finally, I couldn't take it anymore. I decided I had to fix my memory issues and thought that if I got a job that would be the answer.

When I decided to go back to work in 2002 I started part-time as an office manager in a health and wellness massage therapy clinic. Two of my children had severe asthma and numerous allergies from the time they were babies, so wellness had become a big interest in my life. We chose to start using a homeopathic doctor and veered away from traditional medicine, so this job fit perfectly into my life at that time. About a year later, 2003, I was offered another part-time position as a support representative for a staffing agency. I wasn't really looking for another job, but the kids were getting older, and all doing activities which could be expensive, so I ended up accepting the job. Approximately 6 months later I was offered full-time hours with a promotion to service representative and a very nice pay increase. I accepted the offer, but had to give up the position at the Wellness Massage Therapy Clinic. In 2007 I was promoted to Office Manager and stayed in that position until 2010 when I was promoted to Service Supervisor, responsible for all support and service representatives in the company. I attended client meetings, provided training, and travelled to the offices to work with the inside service staff weekly. The company decided to end this position so I returned to manage the office I had previously been managing. In 2013 I was promoted again, this time to Manger of Service Operations where I continued to work until I was downsized in April of 2015.

No matter what position I have had with various companies, as well as in my volunteer work, my passion has always been to educate and mentor. I absolutely love learning, and sharing that knowledge with others. I have been extremely fortunate to have always enjoyed my work and to have been able to do the things I love. As a personal life coach I am able to make a bigger contribution to the lives of the individuals I am fortunate enough to work with. I get a lot of joy from working with my clients and seeing the changes they are able to make happen in their lives.

Personally life becomes so much easier when you have a coach to help you and guide you through life. My coach, Gregory Downey, has been an incredible source of inspiration for me. My wish is that children receive coaching when they start primary school; I believe that they would come out of high school much happier, healthier and more confident individuals if they were able to continue coaching throughout their school careers. Life itself is the biggest, most challenging, exciting activity you will ever participate in, and one of the only few that have no coaching! Hockey, dance, karate, lacrosse, gymnastics, figure skating all require coaching to ensure that you learn the required skills, become continually better, and get the most out of the activity but ...LIFE, the most important of all and the one you only have one chance to get right, you do on your own with no guidance or support. I am offering you a free 15 minute discovery session one on one with me to assist you in Healing Your Way To Happiness. *Please register at www.ijustwanttobehappybook.com.*

Chapter 10

An Unexpected Chance For Change

Being downsized from a job I loved turned out to be one of the best things that could have happened. I must say that the initial shock took a minute to settle in, but almost immediately I saw it as a positive move. I would never have left this job on my own; I would have continued working there until I retired. I liked the work, liked the company, liked the people, and was happy with my compensation. I would not have chosen to give it up on my own so I am grateful to my boss for recognizing something that I couldn't see at the time and thankful for the Universe to provide me with what I needed instead of perhaps what I thought I wanted.

My boss, by letting me go, has improved my life in many ways. I also have to say that he improved my life while I worked for him as well. I would never have imagined receiving the kind of pay I was getting had he not made it possible by seeing my worth and the value I added to him personally and to his company. I would not have had the opportunity to grow my mindset, my skillset, or improve my leadership if he had not given me the opportunities he did. I left his company and his employ with no hard feelings and no regrets. Many people felt that I should be angry and upset after everything I had done for him and his company, but I wasn't. I felt very positive, and was actually excited to have another chance to decide and imagine what I wanted to be when I grew up!

I started looking at various jobs I'd had over the years and dissecting them, analyzing them. I picked the parts of each job that I enjoyed the most and made a list. From there I thought of the various positions that could combine the best and leave out the rest. There really weren't many traditional jobs that fit that mold. Then it hit me; being a life coach was exactly what I was looking for. I started researching coaching businesses. Coaching would give me the opportunity to do what I loved most; to mentor and educate people. This has always been my purpose and my passion. I signed up to be a coaching client and I loved the process as well as the results. I was invited by Achieve Today to become part of their certification program to become a Certified Life Coach. This is definitely a perfect fit for me. I absolutely love coaching clients and assisting them to make positive changes in their lives. I get very excited during each client call, and can feel the passion and joy it brings to me instantly. The hour I spend one on one with a client is one of the best parts in my day, every day. It is a very rewarding experience for the client and for me. As they grow so I continue to grow, improve, and flourish as a coach and a person.

Somehow down deep I think I knew I should be doing something more meaningful with my life. I think that is the reason I was not upset at losing my job and being downsized. Of course, after being accustomed to the pay I had been receiving it was scary to lose the income, but for some reason I felt like everything was going to work out for the best.

Learning to cry may have been the most difficult lesson I have ever learned, and certainly the one I fought hardest against. I have been really uncomfortable with tears for as long as I can remember. I cried very rarely and would get upset with myself if I did have a moment where tears overcame me. For some reason I looked at crying as an act of weakness. I developed this belief after my brother's death and carried it with me throughout my life.

While raising my children I also put this belief onto them. If they were crying because they injured themselves that was okay, but if they were crying because they found something to be upsetting or because they didn't get their own way – not allowed! They had to go to their room until they were able to settle down and communicate rationally. Therefore, I was teaching them to control their emotions, to bury their feelings rather than to accept their emotions and understand their feelings simply because it was easier for me. Of course, at the time I wasn't evolved enough to comprehend what I was encouraging them to become. My youngest daughter was my crier, and I was never really able to break her from that, thankfully. She is certainly the one that is most in touch with her feelings and the most able to express herself emotionally.

Even at work as a leader I made it clear that the workplace was not the place for emotions. People knew that I had no time for whining, and certainly not for crying. I felt that staff should keep their emotions in check while at work, no matter what was causing the feelings to well up inside them. I believed that crying should be done at home, never in the workplace, unless they had suffered severe trauma or the death of a loved one. Even then I really felt that if they could not keep themselves together they should go home and get themselves back together and under control.

I was always stunned when people broke into tears when they were let go from the company as well. No matter how many times I had to let someone go I never got used to the fact that they reacted to the news with tears. In my own defense, I just never thought that losing a job was a big enough life event to deserve tears. I could be empathetic and kind to staff when they were upset; I just could not understand it.

The day I learned to cry was the day I really started to heal. Crying finally released years of suppressed emotions. I was able to see eventually that I was no longer in touch with my own emotions and hadn't been for many, many years. This release finally allowed me to forgive, to let go of some of my deepest fears and to see that I can trust in life. It allowed me to see that my need for control was based out of fear, not strength. I also learned that I am stronger than I believed, but that doesn't mean that I can't feel. Once I was able to cry I realized that laughter came more easily as well. I had been so afraid of falling apart if I allowed myself to feel the sadness within me that I robbed myself of the joy, happiness, forgiveness, peace and prosperity that life has to offer. A huge weight was lifted from my body and soul once I learned how to cry. I felt lighter than I had in a very long time, mentally, physically and emotionally.

You need to free yourself to allow all of your emotions to live a happier, healthier, more balanced life. Accept the emotions that come to you, acknowledge them, let them move through you, and then choose to let them go. Life and how you live it is all a choice, and you are the only person that can make change and choose a new path. It really is that simple – choose to be happy in every moment! *Download a free copy of my "Happiness Handbook" by going to www.ijustwanttobehappybook.com.*

April 28, 2015 gave me an unexpected chance for change. It was a total surprise; I was not expecting to lose my job, at least on a conscious level. However, the previous day in a moment of frustration I stated out loud to myself (and perhaps to the Universe) that "I don't know how much more of this I can take." So at some level I knew that I wasn't doing everything I was meant to be doing with my life. Initially I was shocked, but I accepted the news easily and graciously, gathered my belongings and left the building. The worst was yet to come; my daughter was downsized next. I knew it was coming but was unable to warn her or be there to support her. I waited on the sidewalk outside the building for her to emerge. We drove home, one behind the other. I realized the moment I was let go that there was no way they would keep her on, and that she would be collateral damage, and this is hard for a mother to see. However, I knew this was a risk when she was hired and so it is part of life, and of the reality of business. When the news was released to the staff members many were surprised and in disbelief because things had been going well within the company. My family was also in dismay as they had watched me pour my heart and soul into the company for many years, working long hours, and making many positive changes.

I, however, felt a certain peace and positivity. I was excited to be home for the spring and summer months because I would be able to concentrate on getting the yard work and the house exterior ready for my daughter's wedding the following summer. If I hadn't lost my job I never would have had the energy to get it all done. I worked hard, but the physicality of the work was just what I needed. My mind and body were exhausted from my job so the ability to be outside working in my gardens, which I always found to be relaxing, was just the medicine I needed. In September my husband and I vacationed in Mexico and when we returned I was ready to start something new.

Since April 28, 2015 I have seen many opportunities presented to me that previously I would have dismissed based on my fears. I have learned that no one should have only one income stream as I did previously; if your only income is from your job, then the loss of that job will impact your life greatly. One of my personal goals for 2016 is to have 6 income streams before the end of the year so that I will never again be in the situation of feeling stuck financially, or having to live again in a scarcity mindset.

I had begun working with a life coach in June, and in September I made the decision to become a Certified Life Coach. I felt this is what I needed to do with my life, it was my purpose. I am now able to assist people to live their purpose by helping them to heal their hearts, one person, one day, one step at a time, all over the world. If you feel stuck in your life, if you feel that you are not living to your fullest potential, if you are being held back because of traumatic events that jhappened in your life, if you are feeling depressed, fighting with mental illness, then life coaching may be the step you need to overcome the challenges you are facing each day. Life is like an onion, and once you can begin to peel away the layers and release what's inside, life begins to open up and you will see opportunities that you were unable to see before. *If you are ready for positive change in your life, register for my free 15 minute, one on one discovery session by visiting www.ijustwanttobehappybook.com. I look forward to talking to you and understanding the challenges you are facing.*

I can now say that I have an incredible life. Previously in my writing I found myself saying things like "I know I have a nice life" or "I know I have nothing to complain about" or "I have a great family, a nice home, and friends, and yet something seems to be missing." I always felt guilty, how could I be lucky enough to have all of the people and things I have in my life and yet still feel dissatisfied? Part of what was holding me back was that very guilt, but it went much deeper.

Fear, guilt, mistrust, control; all of these negative emotions were running my life. I was living in a place of negativity even though I was not consciously aware. Every decision I made came from that negativity. I was going against my own inner values, and trying to be someone other than who I was. This place I was living is what I now call "the gap." Living in "the gap" is what causes stress and unhappiness in life. This is how you end up always "chasing." Chasing a relationship, or a better relationship, chasing a new job or career, a better house, a better car, more money, or whatever the case may be for you, it could simply be "keeping up" with friends, family and neighbours. You end up spending your whole life "chasing" things that you think will make you happy. What really happens, though, is you ignore the people and things you already have in your life, including yourself, that could be making you happy right now, or at least used to make you happy. You get so caught up in the "chase" that you forget to appreciate what you have in the moment. Rather than constantly chasing something new, can you imagine what could happen if you put that same time, energy, money and passion into enjoying what you already have? Do you think that perhaps if you could learn to practice gratitude, love, and happiness that your current life could feel so much more enriched?

I know that I often took the people and the things in my life for granted. Once you have won the prize, you have a fleeting moment of pride or happiness, but then it passes quickly and the new shine wears off before you even get it home and you are looking for the next quest of bigger, better, and more impressive. Maybe this time you are "chasing" a raise; yes, a raise would definitely improve your life. Then you get the raise and immediately think of some "thing" the money from the raise could purchase, also to improve your life, and then within a very short time the raise is gone, the money is gone, and the shine has worn off the newest trinket you couldn't live without. Now your "gap" has widened, you feel more stressed, more resentful, you have not improved your lifestyle in any way and you are back at square one starting the "chase" over again! You probably didn't even take time to celebrate the wins either, if you are anything like me. You got the raise, spent the money, felt justified, perhaps had a moment where you felt proud of your accomplishment or happy that you contributed, and then in a blink life was back to normal. *Learn how to set goals, intentions, and take action by using my "How To Create A Vision Board". Download it for free and start using it today. Visit www.ijustwanttobehappy.com to get your free copy.*

Many relationships end for this very reason. I don't know if anyone starting a new relationship sets clear intentions of becoming a better person or assisting their partner in becoming a better person. I am also not aware of couples that choose to create a wonderful relationship, and make their partner feel special, valued and wholly loved each day, especially once the honeymoon period is over. I think most people assume this is what they want, but like many things in our lives, we don't set clear goals and intentions, and we then lose focus. I know that I certainly didn't create that type of relationship goals with my husband, and in fact, I usually pushed him to the back of the line behind the kids, homework, work, extended family needs, and when I finally got to him and was exhausted, assumed he would understand. I have been married over 28 years and as with everything else in my life, our marriage has been good; nothing to complain about at all. We rarely fought, we both did our own thing, but consistently put each other and ourselves last. Neither of us are terribly romantic people by nature so we didn't make time for dating or our relationship. The kids monopolized our time, and we both enjoyed the kids a lot so it never seemed like we were missing out. However, we never made each other a priority and now I think our marriage could have been much happier day to day if we had chosen to put forth some extra effort for each other.

Now I notice that when my energy is low and I'm feeling off, my husband follows suit very quickly, and vice versa. It is still usually his behavior I notice before my own, but it is a good reminder for me to look back at myself. I believe that you see in others what is inside you, so you are projecting out what you see in others. So when I see that my husband is feeling "cranky" it is actually me that is cranky and it is a signal for me to check in with myself to see what is going on with me at that moment. The minute I recognize and then adjust my feelings I can see his mood improve. I find this to be quite funny now because for many years I have found him to be a moody person but in actual fact I was the one creating his moods. When you have the ability to look at a person for the first time, and realize that they are simply reflecting your own energy and emotions back to you, it changes the way you perceive the other person. Now when this happens I no longer feel like his mood is something I have to endure because I now have the awareness and can laugh at myself and at him, choose to change my own mood, and be able to truly enjoy spending time with him. We have had better, and more conversations in the last year than in the previous 26 years. We can even do home renovations together and actually get along, joke around, and enjoy ourselves.

Life coaching has allowed me to finally move past sorrow to joy. I have healed in ways I never knew were possible, and I couldn't have done it on my own because I didn't know what to do, or where to start. I have been able to forgive myself, I have learned to accept emotions as a resource to guide me, I have been able to reduce my fears, clear away hatred, and open myself up to all of the possibilities and opportunities the Universe has to offer. I am able to be free, to be the person I desire to be, to create the changes I want in my life, to learn new things, to acknowledge that I don't have all the answers and I am not expected to. I can dream, I can create, I can love without fear, I can fail, I can succeed, I am worthy, I am smart enough, and I can live the life I choose. I can be happy...that is my right as a human being and no one but me can stop happiness from living within. I choose to be happy! What will you choose?

About the Author

I am many things to many people, including a daughter, a wife, a mother, a sister, a friend, a woman, and a life coach. As long as I can remember, I have been an "educator or mentor" in some way or another. In the end, though, I am me, a woman who is passionate about helping people live a life of fulfillment, happiness and love.

I have always been extremely fortunate to have lived a satisfying life. I have a wonderful husband of 28 years, and four amazing children: 3 daughters and 1 son. We had 4 children in 4 1/2 years, and they are now aged 27, 26, 24, and 22. My family has always been my motivation, and I was born to be a mother, a job I love more than anything in the world! Yet, I felt as though I was meant to do more, to share my experiences with others.

I have suffered heartbreak in my own life on more than one occasion. I learned at the very young age of 5 that once your heart is broken, it will never be quite the same again. For many of us, we carry this emptiness with us for the rest of our lives, and seem to end up living life from the sidelines, afraid of what may happen if we truly engage again.

Yet through all of the sadness I still held a deep belief that things happen in our lives for a specific reason, even if you can't possibly understand what that reason may be at the time. It is this faith that brought me through all of the challenges life has shown me, and it is this faith that has now led me to this point in my life. I am doing the work I have always known I was meant to do and this is the reason I was put on this earth. I believe that I was meant to experience all of the heartbreak in my own life so that I can earnestly and honestly help others heal from theirs.

Heartache can come in many forms, and you can feel the loss very deeply and it can shift through all areas of your life. It shows up in your relationships, your health, your finances, and your business or career. How you handle the after effects is your choice, and you can continue to live with the sadness or you can choose to change your reality; the choice is up to you!